NIST Special Publication 800-56A

March, 2007

NIST

**National Institute of
Standards and Technology**

Recommendation for Pair-Wise
Key Establishment Schemes
Using Discrete Logarithm
Cryptography

(Revised)

Elaine Barker, Don Johnson, and Miles Smid

C O M P U T E R   S E C U R I T Y

Abstract

This Recommendation specifies key establishment schemes using discrete logarithm cryptography, based on standards developed by the Accredited Standards Committee (ASC) X9, Inc.: ANS X9.42 (*Agreement of Symmetric Keys Using Discrete Logarithm Cryptography*) and ANS X9.63 (*Key Agreement and Key Transport Using Elliptic Curve Cryptography*).

KEY WORDS: assurances; Diffie-Hellman; elliptic curve cryptography; finite field cryptography; key agreement; key confirmation; key derivation; key establishment; key management; key recovery; key transport; MQV.

Acknowledgements

The National Institute of Standards and Technology (NIST) gratefully acknowledges and appreciates contributions by Rich Davis, Mike Hopper and Laurie Law from the National Security Agency concerning the many security issues associated with this Recommendation. NIST also thanks the many contributions by the public and private sectors whose thoughtful and constructive comments improved the quality and usefulness of this publication.

Authority

This document has been developed by the National Institute of Standards and Technology (NIST) in furtherance of its statutory responsibilities under the Federal Information Security Management Act (FISMA) of 2002, Public Law 107-347.

NIST is responsible for developing standards and guidelines, including minimum requirements, for providing adequate information security for all agency operations and assets, but such standards and guidelines shall not apply to national security systems. This guideline is consistent with the requirements of the Office of Management and Budget (OMB) Circular A-130, Section 8b(3), Securing Agency Information Systems, as analyzed in A-130, Appendix IV: Analysis of Key Sections. Supplemental information is provided in A-130, Appendix III.

This Recommendation has been prepared for use by federal agencies. It may be used by nongovernmental organizations on a voluntary basis and is not subject to copyright. (Attribution would be appreciated by NIST.)

Nothing in this document should be taken to contradict standards and guidelines made mandatory and binding on federal agencies by the Secretary of Commerce under statutory authority. Nor should these guidelines be interpreted as altering or superseding the existing authorities of the Secretary of Commerce, Director of the OMB, or any other federal official.

Conformance testing for implementations of key establishment schemes, as specified in this Recommendation, will be conducted within the framework of the Cryptographic Module Validation Program (CMVP), a joint effort of NIST and the Communications Security Establishment of the Government of Canada. An implementation of a key establishment scheme must adhere to the requirements in this Recommendation in order to be validated under the CMVP. The requirements of this Recommendation are indicated by the word "shall."

Table of Contents

Figures

Tables

1.   Introduction

Many U.S. Government Information Technology (IT) systems need to employ well-established cryptographic schemes to protect the integrity and confidentiality of the data that they process. Algorithms such as the Advanced Encryption Standard (AES) as defined in Federal Information Processing Standard (FIPS) 197, Triple DES as specified in NIST Special Publication (SP) 800-67, and HMAC as defined in FIPS 198 make attractive choices for the provision of these services. These algorithms have been standardized to facilitate interoperability between systems. However, the use of these algorithms requires the establishment of shared secret keying material in advance. Trusted couriers may manually distribute this secret keying material. However, as the number of entities using a system grows, the work involved in the distribution of the secret keying material could grow rapidly. Therefore, it is essential to support the cryptographic algorithms used in modern U.S. Government applications with automated key establishment schemes.

2.   Scope and Purpose

This Recommendation provides the specifications of key establishment schemes that are appropriate for use by the U.S. Federal Government, based on standards developed by the Accredited Standards Committee (ASC) X9, Inc.: ANS X9.42 *Agreement of Symmetric Keys using Discrete Logarithm Cryptography* and ANS X9.63 *Key Agreement and Key Transport using Elliptic Curve Cryptography*. A key establishment scheme can be characterized as either a key agreement scheme or a key transport scheme. The asymmetric-key-based key agreement schemes in this Recommendation are based on the Diffie-Hellman (DH) and Menezes-Qu-Vanstone (MQV) algorithms. In addition, an asymmetric-key-based key transport scheme is specified. It is intended that an adjunct key establishment schemes Recommendation will contain key transport scheme(s) from ANS X9.44 *Key Agreement and Key Transport using Factoring-Based Cryptography,* when they become available.

This Recommendation provides a description of selected schemes from ANS X9 standards. When there are differences between this Recommendation and the referenced ANS X9 standards, this key establishment schemes Recommendation **shall** have precedence for U.S. Government applications.

This Recommendation is intended for use in conjunction with NIST Special Publication 800-57, *Recommendation for Key Management* [7]. This key establishment schemes Recommendation, the Recommendation for Key Management [7], and the referenced ANS X9 standards are intended to provide sufficient information for a vendor to implement secure key establishment using asymmetric algorithms in FIPS 140-2 [1] validated modules.

A scheme may be a component of a protocol, which in turn provides additional security properties not provided by the scheme when considered by itself. Note that protocols, per se, are not specified in this Recommendation.

3. Definitions, Symbols and Abbreviations

3.1 Definitions

Approved	FIPS approved or NIST Recommended. An algorithm or technique that is either 1) specified in a FIPS or NIST Recommendation, or 2) adopted in a FIPS or NIST Recommendation and specified either (a) in an appendix to the FIPS or NIST Recommendation, or (b) in a document referenced by the FIPS or NIST Recommendation.
Assurance of identifier	Confidence that identifying information (such as a name) is correctly associated with an entity.
Assurance of possession of a private key	Confidence that an entity possesses a private key associated with a public key.
Assurance of validity	Confidence that either a key or a set of domain parameters is arithmetically correct.
Bit length	The length in bits of a bit string.
Certification Authority (CA)	The entity in a Public Key Infrastructure (PKI) that is responsible for issuing public key certificates and exacting compliance to a PKI policy.
Cofactor	The order of the elliptic curve group divided by the (prime) order of the generator point specified in the domain parameters.
Domain parameters	The parameters used with a cryptographic algorithm that are common to a domain of users.
Entity	An individual (person), organization, device, or process. "Party" is a synonym.
Ephemeral key	A key that is intended for a very short period of use. The key is ordinarily used in exactly one transaction of a cryptographic scheme; an exception to this is when the ephemeral key is used in multiple transactions for a key transport broadcast. Contrast with static key.

Hash function	A function that maps a bit string of arbitrary length to a fixed length bit string. Approved hash functions satisfy the following properties: 1. (One-way) It is computationally infeasible to find any input that maps to any pre-specified output, and 2. (Collision resistant) It is computationally infeasible to find any two distinct inputs that map to the same output. Approved hash functions are specified in FIPS 180-2 [2].
Identifier	A bit string that is associated with a person, device or organization. It may be an identifying name, or may be something more abstract (for example, a string consisting of an IP address and timestamp). If a party owns a static key pair that is used in a key agreement transaction, then the identifier assigned to that party is one that is bound to that static key pair. If the party does not contribute a static public key as part of a key agreement transaction, then the identifier of that party is a non-null identifier selected in accordance with the protocol utilizing the scheme.
Initiator	The party that begins a key agreement transaction. Contrast with responder.
Key agreement	A key establishment procedure where the resultant secret keying material is a function of information contributed by two participants, so that no party can predetermine the value of the secret keying material independently from the contributions of the other parties. Contrast with key transport.
Key agreement transaction	The instance that results in shared secret keying material among different parties using a key agreement scheme.
Key confirmation	A procedure to provide assurance to one party (the key confirmation recipient) that another party (the key confirmation provider) actually possesses the correct secret keying material and/or shared secret.
Key derivation	The process by which keying material is derived from a shared secret and other information.
Key establishment	The procedure that results in shared secret keying material among different parties.

Key establishment transaction	An instance of establishing secret keying material using a key establishment scheme.
Key transport	A key establishment procedure whereby one party (the sender) selects a value for the secret keying material and then securely distributes that value to another party (the receiver). Contrast with key agreement.
Key transport transaction	The instance that results in shared secret keying material between different parties using a key transport scheme.
Key wrap	A method of encrypting keying material (along with associated integrity information) that provides both confidentiality and integrity protection using a symmetric key algorithm.
Keying material	The data that is necessary to establish and maintain a cryptographic keying relationship. Some keying material may be secret, while other keying material may be public. As used in this Recommendation, secret keying material may include keys, secret initialization vectors or other secret information; public keying material includes any non-secret data needed to establish a relationship.
MacTag	Data that allows an entity to verify the integrity of the information. Other documents sometimes refer to this data as a MAC.
Message Authentication Code (MAC) algorithm	Defines a family of one-way cryptographic functions that is parameterized by a symmetric key and produces a *MacTag* on arbitrary data. A MAC algorithm can be used to provide data origin authentication as well as data integrity. In this Recommendation, a MAC algorithm is used for key confirmation and validation testing purposes.
Nonce	A time-varying value that has at most a negligible chance of repeating, for example, a random value that is generated anew for each use, a timestamp, a sequence number, or some combination of these.
Owner	For a static key pair, the owner is the entity that is authorized to use the static private key associated with a public key, whether that entity generated the static key pair itself or a trusted party generated the key pair for the entity. For an ephemeral key pair, the owner is the entity that generated the key pair.
Party	An individual (person), organization, device, or process. "Entity" is a synonym for party.

Provider	The party during key confirmation that provides assurance to the other party (the recipient) that the two parties have indeed established a shared secret.
Public key certificate	A set of data that contains an entity's identifier(s), the entity's public key (including an indication of the associated set of domain parameters, if any) and possibly other information, and is digitally signed by a trusted party, thereby binding the public key to the included identifier(s).
Receiver	The party that receives secret keying material via a key transport transaction. Contrast with sender.
Recipient	A party that receives (1) keying material: such as a static public key (e.g., in a certificate) or an ephemeral public key; (2) assurance: such as an assurance of the validity of a candidate public key or assurance of possession of the private key associated with a public key; or (3) key confirmation. Contrast with provider.
Responder	The party that does not begin a key agreement transaction. Contrast with initiator.
Scheme	A (cryptographic) scheme consists of an unambiguous specification of a set of transformations that are capable of providing a (cryptographic) service when properly implemented and maintained. A scheme is a higher level construct than a primitive and a lower level construct than a protocol.
Security strength (Also "Bits of security")	A number associated with the amount of work (that is, the number of operations) that is required to break a cryptographic algorithm or system.
Security properties	The security features (e.g., entity authentication, playback protection, or key confirmation) that a cryptographic scheme may, or may not, provide.
Sender	The party that sends secret keying material to the receiver using a key transport transaction.
Shall	This term is used to indicate a requirement of a Federal Information processing Standard (FIPS) or a requirement that needs to be fulfilled to claim conformance to this Recommendation. Note that **shall** may be coupled with **not** to become **shall not**.

Shared secret keying material	The secret keying material that is either (1) derived by applying the key derivation function to the shared secret and other shared information during a key agreement process, or (2) is transported during a key transport process.
Shared secret	A secret value that has been computed using a key agreement scheme and is used as input to a key derivation function.
Should	This term is used to indicate an important recommendation. Ignoring the recommendation could result in undesirable results. Note that **should** may be coupled with **not** to become **should not**.
Static key	A key that is intended for use for a relatively long period of time and is typically intended for use in many instances of a cryptographic key establishment scheme. Contrast with an ephemeral key.
Symmetric key algorithm	A cryptographic algorithm that uses one secret key that is shared between authorized parties.
Trusted party	A trusted party is a party that is trusted by an entity to faithfully perform certain services for that entity. An entity may choose to act as a trusted party for itself.
Trusted third party	A third party, such as a CA, that is trusted by its clients to perform certain services. (By contrast, the initiator and responder in a scheme are considered to be the first and second parties in a key establishment transaction.)

3.2   Symbols and Abbreviations

General:

AES	Advanced Encryption Standard (as specified in FIPS 197 [4]).
ASC	The American National Standards Institute (ANSI) Accredited Standards Committee.
ANS	American National Standard.
ASN.1	Abstract Syntax Notation One.
CA	Certification Authority.

CDH	The cofactor Diffie-Hellman key agreement primitive.
DH	The (non-cofactor) Diffie-Hellman key agreement primitive.
DLC	Discrete Logarithm Cryptography, which is comprised of both Finite Field Cryptography (FFC) and Elliptic Curve Cryptography (ECC).
EC	Elliptic Curve.
ECC	Elliptic Curve Cryptography, the public key cryptographic methods using an elliptic curve. For example, see ANS X9.63 [12].
FF	Finite Field.
FFC	Finite Field Cryptography, the public key cryptographic methods using a finite field. For example, see ANS X9.42 [10].
HMAC	Keyed-hash Message Authentication Code (as specified in FIPS 198 [5]).
ID	The bit string denoting the identifier associated with an entity.
H	An Approved hash function.
KC	Key Confirmation.
KDF	Key Derivation Function.
MAC	Message Authentication Code.
MQV	The Menezes-Qu-Vanstone key agreement primitive.
Null	The empty bit string
SHA	Secure Hash Algorithm.
TTP	A Trusted Third Party.
U	The initiator of a key establishment process.
V	The responder in a key establishment process.
{X}	Indicates that the inclusion of X is optional.

$X \parallel Y$	Concatenation of two strings X and Y.
$\lvert x \rvert$	The length of x in bits.
$[a, b]$	The set of integers x such that $a \leq x \leq b$.
$\lceil x \rceil$	The ceiling of x; the smallest integer $\geq x$. For example, $\lceil 5 \rceil = 5$, $\lceil 5.3 \rceil = 6$.

The following notations for FFC and ECC are consistent with those used in the ANS X9.42 and ANS X9.63 standards; however, it should be recognized that the notation between the standards is inconsistent (for example, x and y are used as the private and public keys in ANS X9.42, whereas x and y are used as the coordinates of a point in ANS X9.63).

FFC (ANS X9.42):

g	An FFC domain parameter; the generator of the subgroup of order q.
mod p	The reduction modulo p of an integer value.
p	An FFC domain parameter; the (large) prime field order.
pgenCounter	An FFC domain parameter, a value that may be output during domain parameter generation to provide assurance at a later time that the resulting domain parameters were generated arbitrarily.
q	An FFC domain parameter; the (small) prime multiplicative subgroup order.
r_U, r_V	Party U or Party V's ephemeral private key. These are integers in the range $[1, q\text{-}1]$.
t_U, t_V	Party U or Party V's ephemeral public key. These are integers in the range $[2, p\text{-}2]$, representing elements in the finite field of size p.
SEED	An FFC domain parameter; an initialization value that is used during domain parameter generation that can also be used to provide assurance at a later time that the resulting domain parameters were generated arbitrarily.
x_U, x_V	Party U or Party V's static private key. These are integers in the range $[1, q\text{-}1]$.
y_U, y_V	Party U or Party V's static public key. These are integers in the range $[2, p\text{-}2]$, representing elements in the finite field of size p.

Z	A shared secret that is used to derive secret keying material using a key derivation function.
Z_e	An ephemeral shared secret that is computed using the Diffie-Hellman primitive.
Z_s	A static shared secret that is computed using the Diffie-Hellman primitive.

ECC (ANS X9.63):

a, b	An ECC domain parameter; two field elements that define the equation of an elliptic curve.
avf(Q)	The associate value of the elliptic curve point Q.
$d_{e,U}, d_{e,V}$	Party U's and Party V's ephemeral private keys. These are integers in the range $[1, n\text{-}1]$.
$d_{s,U}, d_{s,V}$	Party U's and Party V's static private keys. These are integers in the range $[1, n\text{-}1]$.
FR	Field Representation indicator. An indication of the basis used for representing field elements. FR is NULL if the field has odd prime order or if a Gaussian normal basis is used. If a polynomial basis representation is used for a field of order 2^m, then FR is the reduction polynomial (a trinomial or a pentanomial). See [12] for details.
G	An ECC domain parameter, which is a distinguished point on an elliptic curve that generates the subgroup of order n.
h	An ECC domain parameter, the cofactor, which is the order of the elliptic curve divided by the order of the point G.
n	An ECC domain parameter; the order of the point G.
O	The point at infinity; a special point in an elliptic curve group that serves as the (additive) identity.
q	An ECC domain parameter; the field size.
$Q_{e,U}, Q_{e,V}$	Party U's and Party V's ephemeral public keys. These are points on the elliptic curve defined by the domain parameters.

$Q_{s,U}, Q_{s,V}$	Party U's and Party V's static public keys. These are points on the elliptic curve defined by the domain parameters.
SEED	An ECC domain parameter; an initialization value that is used during domain parameter generation that can also be used to provide assurance at a later time that the resulting domain parameters were generated arbitrarily.
x_P, y_P	Elements of the finite field of size q, representing the x and y coordinates, respectively, of a point P. These are integers in the interval $[0, p\text{-}1]$ in the case that q is an odd prime p, or are bit strings of length m bits in the case that $q = 2^m$.
Z	A shared secret that is used to derive secret keying material using a key derivation function.
Z_e	An ephemeral shared secret that is computed using the Diffie-Hellman primitive.
Z_s	A static shared secret that is computed using the Diffie-Hellman primitive.

4.   Key Establishment Schemes Overview

Secret cryptographic keying material may be electronically established between parties by using a key establishment scheme, that is, by using either a key agreement scheme or a key transport scheme.

During key agreement (where both parties contribute to the shared secret and, therefore, the derived secret keying material), the secret keying material to be established is not sent directly; rather, information is exchanged between both parties that allows each party to derive the secret keying material. Key agreement schemes may use either symmetric key or asymmetric key (public key) techniques. The key agreement schemes described in this Recommendation use public key techniques. The party that begins a key agreement scheme is called the initiator, and the other party is called the responder.

During key transport (where one party selects the secret keying material), wrapped (that is, encrypted) secret keying material is transported from the sender to the receiver. Key transport schemes may use either symmetric key or public key techniques; only key transport schemes based on Discrete Logarithm Cryptography (DLC) cryptography are described in this Recommendation. The party that sends the secret keying material is called the sender, and the other party is called the receiver.

The security of the DLC schemes in this Recommendation is based on the intractability of the discrete logarithm problem. The schemes calculated over a finite field (FF) are based on ANS X9.42. The schemes calculated using elliptic curves (EC) are based on ANS X9.63.

This Recommendation specifies several processes that are associated with key establishment (including processes for generating domain parameters and for deriving secret keying material from a shared secret). In each case, equivalent processes may be used. Two processes are equivalent if, when the same values are input to each process (either as input parameters or as values made available during the process), the same output is produced. Some processes are used to provide assurance (for example, assurance of the arithmetic validity of a public key or assurance of possession of a private key associated with a public key). The party that provides the assurance is called the provider (of the assurance), and the other party is called the recipient (of the assurance).

Note that the terms initiator, responder, sender, receiver, provider and recipient have specific meanings in this Recommendation.

A number of steps are performed to establish secret keying material as described in Sections 4.1 and 4.2.

4.1   Key Agreement Preparations by an Owner

The owner of a private/public key pair is the entity that is authorized to use the private key of that key pair. Figure 1 depicts the steps that may be required of that entity when preparing for a key agreement process.

The first step is to obtain appropriate domain parameters that are generated as specified in Section 5.5.1; either the entity itself generates the domain parameters, or the entity obtains domain parameters that another entity has generated. Having obtained the domain parameters, the entity obtains assurance of the validity of those domain parameters; approved methods for obtaining this assurance are provided in Section 5.5.2.

If the entity will be using a key establishment scheme that requires that the entity have a static key pair, the entity obtains this key pair. Either the entity generates the key pair as specified in Section 5.6.1 or a trusted party generates the key pair as specified in Section 5.6.1 and provides it to the entity. The entity (i.e., the owner) obtains assurance of the validity of its static public key and also obtains assurance that it actually possesses the (correct) static private key. Approved methods for obtaining assurance of public key validity by the owner are addressed in Section 5.6.2.1; approved methods for an owner to obtain assurance of the actual possession of the private key are provided in Section 5.6.3.1.

An *identifier* (see Section 3.1) is used to label the entity that is authorized to use the static private key corresponding to a particular static public key (i.e., the identifier labels the key pair's owner). This label may uniquely distinguish the entity from all others, in which case it could rightfully be considered an identity. However, the label may be something less specific – an organization, nickname, etc. – hence, the term *identifier* is used in this Recommendation, rather than the term *identity*. A key pair's owner is responsible for ensuring that the identifier associated with its static public key is appropriate for the applications in which it will be used.

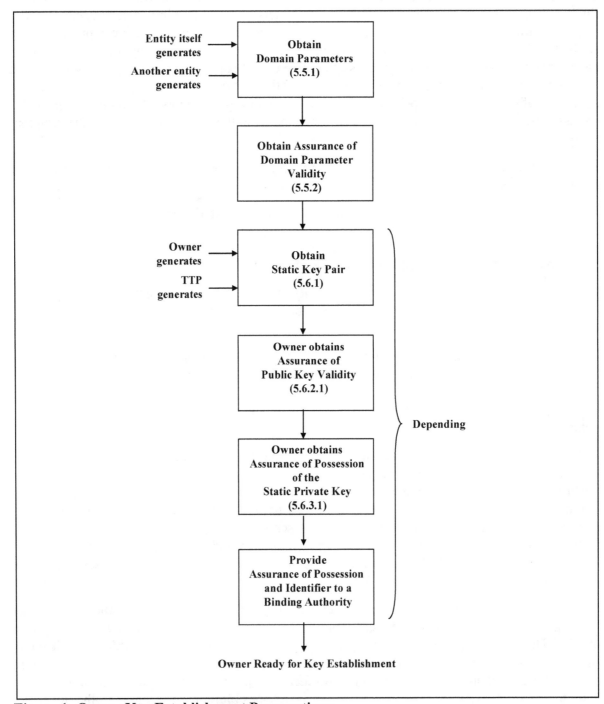

Figure 1: Owner Key Establishment Preparations

This Recommendation assumes that there is a trustworthy binding of each entity's identifier to the entity's static public key. The binding of an identifier to a static public key may be accomplished by a trusted authority (i.e., a binding authority; for example, a registration authority working with a CA who creates a certificate containing both the static public key and the identifier). The binding authority verifies the identifier chosen for the owner. The binding authority is also responsible for obtaining assurance of: the validity of the domain parameters associated with the owner's key pair, the arithmetic validity of the owner's static public key, and the owner's possession of the static private key corresponding to that static public key. (See, for example, Section 5.5.2, Section 5.6.2.2 [method 1], and Section 5.6.3.2.2, where the binding authority acts as the recipient of the static public key.) Binding Authorities **shall** obtain assurance of possession either by using one of the methods specified in Section 5.6.3.2.2 or by using an Approved alternative.

After the above steps have been performed, the entity (i.e., the static key pair owner) is ready to enter into a key establishment process with another compatibly prepared entity.

4.2   Key Agreement Process

Figure 2 depicts the steps that may be required of an entity when establishing secret keying material with another entity using one of the key agreement schemes described in this Recommendation; however, some discrepancies in order may occur, depending on the communication protocol in which the key agreement process is performed. Depending on the key agreement scheme and the available keys, either entity could be the key agreement initiator. Note that some of the shown actions may not be a part of some schemes. For example, key confirmation is optional (see Section 8). The specifications of this recommendation indicate when a particular action is required.

Each entity obtains the identifier associated with the other entity, and verifies that the identifier of the other entity corresponds to the entity with whom the participant wishes to establish secret keying material.

Each entity that requires the other entity's static public key for use in the key establishment scheme obtains that public key and obtains assurance of its validity. Approved methods for obtaining assurance of the validity of a static public key are provided in Section 5.6.2.2.

Each entity that requires the other entity's ephemeral public key for use in the key establishment scheme obtains that public key and obtains assurance of its validity. Ephemeral key pairs are generated as specified in Section 5.6.1; the ephemeral private key is not provided to the other entity. Approved methods for obtaining assurance of the validity of an ephemeral public key are provided in Section 5.6.2.3.

If the key agreement scheme requires that an entity provide a nonce, the nonce is generated as specified in Section 5.4 and provided to the other entity.

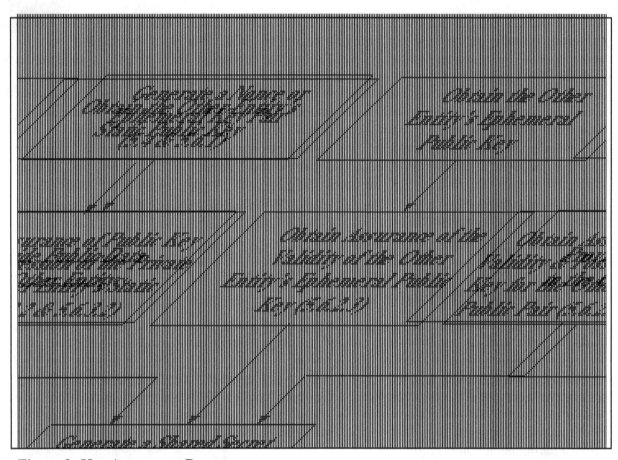

Figure 2: Key Agreement Process

If one or both of the participants wish to confirm that the other entity has computed the same shared secret or the same secret keying material as part of the key agreement process, key confirmation is performed as specified in Section 8.4.

Assurance of static private key possession is obtained prior to using the derived keying material for purposes beyond those of the key agreement transaction itself (see Section 5.6.3.2).

4.3   DLC-based Key Transport Process

Figure 3 depicts the steps that are performed when transporting secret keying material from one entity to another using a key transport scheme. Depending on the available keys, either entity could be the key transport sender. Prior to performing key transport, a key-wrapping key is established by using a key agreement process as specified in Section 7. Key confirmation may be performed to obtain assurance that both parties possess the same key-wrapping key. The sender selects secret keying material to be sent to the other entity, wraps the keying material using the key-wrapping key and sends the wrapped keying material to the other entity. The receiving entity receives the wrapped keying material and unwraps it using the previously established key-wrapping key.

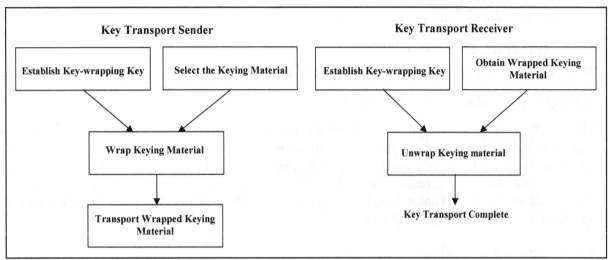

Figure 3: Key Transport Process

5. Cryptographic Elements

This section describes the basic computations that are performed and the assurances that need to be obtained when performing DLC based key establishment. The schemes described in Section 6 are based upon the correct implementation of these computations and assurances.

Tables 1 and 2 of Section 5.5 list parameter size sets to be used in the selection of cryptographic elements. All cryptographic elements used together **shall** be selected in accordance with the same parameter size set.

5.1 Cryptographic Hash Functions

An Approved hash function **shall** be used when a hash function is required (for example, for the key derivation function or to compute a MAC when HMAC, as specified in FIPS 198, is used). FIPS 180-2 [2] specifies Approved hash functions. The hash function **shall** be selected in accordance with the parameter lists in Tables 1 and 2 of Section 5.5.

5.2 Message Authentication Code (MAC) Algorithm

A Message Authentication Code (MAC) algorithm defines a family of one-way (MAC) functions that is parameterized by a symmetric key. In key establishment schemes, an entity is sometimes required to compute a *MacTag* on received or derived data using the MAC function determined by a symmetric key derived from a shared secret. The *MacTag* is sent to another entity in order to confirm that the shared secret was correctly computed. An Approved MAC algorithm **shall** be used to compute a *MacTag*, for example, HMAC [5].

The MAC algorithm is used to provide key confirmation as specified in this Recommendation when key confirmation is desired, and is used to validate implementations of the key establishment schemes specified in this Recommendation (see Section 5.2.3). *MacTag* computation and checking are defined in Sections 5.2.1 and 5.2.2 of this Recommendation.

5.2.1 *MacTag* Computation

The computation of the *MacTag* is represented as follows:

MacTag = MAC(*MacKey*, *MacLen*, *MacData*).

The *MacTag* computation **shall** be performed using an Approved MAC algorithm. In the above equation, MAC represents an Approved MAC algorithm; *MacKey* represents a symmetric key obtained from the *DerivedKeyingMaterial* (see Section 5.8); *MacLen* represents the length of *MacTag;* and *MacData* represents the data on which the *MacTag* is computed. The minimum for *MacLen* is specified in Tables 1 and 2 of Section 5.5. The minimum size for *MacKey* is also specified in Tables 1 and 2. See [5] and [6].

5.2.2 *MacTag* Checking

To check a received *MacTag* (e.g., received during key confirmation and/or implementation validation), a new *MacTag* is computed—using the values of *MacKey*, *MacLen*, and *MacData* possessed by the recipient (as specified in Section 5.2.1). The new *MacTag* is compared with the received *MacTag*. If their values are equal, then it may be inferred that the same *MacKey*, *MacLen*, and *MacData* values were used in the two *MacTag* computations.

5.2.3 Implementation Validation Message

For purposes of validating an implementation of the schemes in this Recommendation during an implementation validation test (under the NIST Cryptographic Validation Program), the value of *MacData* **shall** be the string "Standard Test Message", followed by a 16-byte field for a nonce. The default value for this field is all binary zeros. Different values for this field will be specified during testing. This is for the purposes of testing when no key confirmation capability exists (see Section 10).

Note: ANS X9.42 defines *MacData* as "ANSI X9.42 Testing Message". ANS X9.63 does not address implementation validation at this level of detail. The implementation test message used for NIST validation is a different text string from the implementation test message for ANS X9.42 validation.

5.3 Random Number Generation

Whenever this Recommendation requires the use of a randomly generated value (for example, for keys or nonces), the values **shall** be generated using an Approved random bit generator (RBG) providing an appropriate security strength.

5.4   Nonces

A nonce is a time-varying value that has (at most) a negligible chance of repeating. For example, a nonce may be composed of one (or more) of the following components:

1. A random value that is generated anew for each nonce, using an Approved random bit generator. The security strength of the random bit generator and the entropy of the nonce **shall** be at least one half of the minimum required bit length of the subgroup order (as specified in Tables 1 and 2 of Section 5.5). A nonce containing a component of this type is called a *random nonce*.

2. A timestamp of sufficient resolution (detail) so that it is different each time it is used.

3. A monotonically increasing sequence number, or

4. A combination of a timestamp and a monotonically increasing sequence number such that the sequence number is reset only when the timestamp changes. (For example, a timestamp may show the date but not the time of day, so a sequence number is appended that will not repeat during a particular day.)

Nonces are used, for example, in implementation validation testing (Section 5.2.3), in C(0, 2) schemes (Section 6.3), and in key confirmation (Section 8).

When using a nonce, a random nonce **should** be used.

5.5   Domain Parameters

Discrete Logarithm Cryptography (DLC), which includes Finite Field Cryptography (FFC) and Elliptic Curve Cryptography (ECC), requires that the public and private key pairs be generated with respect to a particular set of domain parameters. A candidate set of domain parameters is said to be valid when it conforms to all the requirements specified in this Recommendation. A user of a candidate set of domain parameters (for example, either an initiator or a responder) **shall** have assurance of domain parameter validity prior to using them. Although domain parameters are public information, they **shall** be managed so that the correct correspondence between a given key pair and its set of domain parameters is maintained for all parties that use the key pair. Domain parameters may remain fixed for an extended time period, and one set of domain parameters may be used with multiple key pairs and with multiple key establishment schemes.

Some schemes in ANS X9.42 and X9.63 allow the set of domain parameters used and associated with static keys to be different from the set of domain parameters used and associated with ephemeral keys. For this Recommendation, however, only one set of domain parameters **shall** be used during any key establishment transaction using a given run of a scheme (that is, the static-key domain parameters and the ephemeral-key domain parameters used in one scheme **shall** be the same).

5.5.1 Domain Parameter Generation

5.5.1.1 FFC Domain Parameter Generation

Domain parameters for FFC schemes are of the form (p, q, g\{, *SEED, pgenCounter*\}), where p is the (larger) prime field order, q is the (smaller) prime (multiplicative) subgroup order, g is a generator of the q-order cyclic subgroup of *GF(p)**, and *SEED* and *pgenCounter* are optional values used in the canonical process of generating and validating p and q, and possibly g, depending on the method of generation. FFC Domain parameters **shall** be generated using a method specified in FIPS 186-3 [3] based on a parameter size set selected from Table 1.

Table 1: FFC Parameter Size Sets

FFC Parameter Set Name	FA	FB	FC
Bit length of field order p (i.e., $\lceil \log_2 p \rceil$)	1024	2048	2048[1]
Bit length of subgroup order q (i.e., $\lceil \log_2 q \rceil$)	160	224	256
Minimum bit length of the hash function output	160	224	256
Minimum MAC key size (for use in key confirmation)	80	112	128
Minimum *MacLen* (for use in key confirmation)	80	112	128

As shown in Table 1, there are three parameter size sets (named FA through FC) for FFC; all the parameters of a particular set **shall** be used together. For U.S. government applications, one or more sets **shall** be selected based on the solution requirements. See the comparable security table in the Recommendation for Key Management [7] to assess the comparable security of any particular parameter size set. The Recommendation for Key Management [7] provides guidance on selecting an appropriate security strength and an appropriate FFC parameter set. If the appropriate security strength does not have an FFC parameter set, then Elliptic Curve Cryptography **should** be used (see Section 5.5.1.2).

For this Recommendation, the size of p (public key size) is a multiple of 1024 bits; the exact length depends on the FFC parameter set selected. For this Recommendation, the size of q is a specific bit length depending on the FFC parameter set selected.

---

[1] Parameter size set FC is included with the same field order length as set FB to allow finite field applications with a 2048-bit field order to have the option of increasing the private key size to 256 bits without having to increase the field order (a more substantial change). FC is not intended to provide more security than FB.

5.5.1.2 ECC Domain Parameter Generation

Domain parameters for ECC schemes are of the form $(q, FR, a, b\{, SEED\}, G, n, h)$, where q is the field size; FR is an indication of the basis used; a and b are two field elements that define the equation of the curve; $SEED$ is an optional bit string that is included if the elliptic curve was randomly generated in a verifiable fashion; G is a generating point (possibly generated from the $SEED$) consisting of (x_G, y_G) of prime order on the curve; n is the order of the point G; and h is the cofactor (which is equal to the order of the curve divided by n). Note that the field size q may be either an odd prime p or 2^m, where m is a prime.

Table 2: ECC Parameter Size Sets

ECC Parameter Set Name	EA	EB	EC	ED	EE
Bit length of ECC subgroup order n (i.e., $\lceil \log_2 n \rceil$)	160-223	224-255	256-383	384-511	512+
Maximum bit length of ECC cofactor h	10	14	16	24	32
Minimum bit length of the hash function output	160	224	256	384	512
Minimum MAC key size (for use in key confirmation)	80	112	128	192	256
Minimum *MacLen* (for use in key confirmation)	80	112	128	192	256

As shown in Table 2, there are five parameter size sets (named EA, EB, EC, ED and EE) for ECC; all the members of a particular set **shall** be used together. For U.S. government applications, one or more sets **shall** be selected based on the solution requirements. See the comparable security table in the Recommendation for Key Management [7] to assess the comparable security of any particular parameter size set. The Recommendation for Key Management [7] provides guidance on selecting the appropriate security strength and an appropriate ECC key size.

The five different cofactor maximums each ensure that the subgroup of order n is unique and that cofactor multiplication is reasonably efficient. The ECC domain parameters **shall** either be generated as specified in ANS X9.62 [13] or selected from the recommended elliptic curve domain parameters specified in FIPS 186-3 [3]. (Note: ANS X9.62, rather than ANS X9.63, specifies the most current method of generating ECC domain parameters at the time of writing this Recommendation.)

5.5.2 Assurances of Domain Parameter Validity

Secure key establishment depends on the arithmetic validity of the set of domain parameters used by the parties. Each party **shall** have assurance of the validity of a candidate set of domain parameters. Each party **shall** obtain assurance that the candidate set of domain parameters is valid in at least one of the following three ways:

1. The party itself generates the set of domain parameters according to the requirements specified in Section 5.5.1.

2. The party performs an explicit domain parameter validation as specified in:

    a. FIPS 186-3 for FFC based on a parameter size set selected from Table 1.

    b. ANS X9.62-2 for ECC.

3. The party has received assurance from a trusted third party (for example, a CA or NIST[2]) that the set of domain parameters was valid at the time that they were generated by reason of either method 1 or 2 above.

    Note: Some domain parameters have been generated using SHA-1, and SHA-1 will be required during their validation. At some time in the future, it is expected that SHA-1 will no longer be an Approved hash function. However, if a set of domain parameters was successfully validated with SHA-1 while it was still an Approved hash function, then those domain parameters will continue to qualify as valid even after the use of SHA-1 is no longer Approved. In particular, this is true of the NIST Recommended Elliptic Curves.

The application performing the key establishment on behalf of the party **should** determine whether or not to allow key establishment based upon the method(s) of assurance that was used. Such knowledge may be explicitly provided to the application in some manner, or may be implicitly provided by the operation of the application itself.

5.5.3 Domain Parameter Management

A particular set of domain parameters **shall** be protected against modification or substitution until the set is deactivated (if and when it is no longer needed). Each private/public key pair **shall** be correctly associated with its specific set of domain parameters.

5.6 Private and Public Keys

This section specifies requirements for the generation of key pairs, assurances of public key validity, assurances of private key possession, and key pair management.

---

[2] If using an elliptic curve from the list of NIST recommended curves in FIPS 186-3 [3].

5.6.1 Private/Public Key Pair Generation

5.6.1.1 FFC Key Pair Generation

For the FFC schemes, each static and ephemeral private key and public key **shall** be generated using an Approved method and the selected valid domain parameters (p, q, g\{, *SEED*, *pgenCounter*\}) (see Appendix B of FIPS 186-3). Each private key **shall** be unpredictable and **shall** be generated in the range [1, q-1] using an Approved random bit generator. The static public key y is computed from the static private key x by using the following formula: $y = g^x$ mod p. Similarly the ephemeral public key t is computed from the ephemeral private key r by using the following formula: $t = g^r$ mod p.

5.6.1.2 ECC Key Pair Generation

For the ECC schemes, each static and ephemeral private key d and public key Q **shall** be generated using an Approved method and the selected domain parameters (q, *FR*, a, b\{, *SEED*\}, G, n, h) (see Appendix B of FIPS 186-3). Each private key, d, **shall** be unpredictable and **shall** be generated in the range [1, n-1] using an Approved random bit generator. The public key Q is computed by using the following formula: $Q = (x_Q, y_Q) = dG$.

5.6.2 Assurances of the Arithmetic Validity of a Public Key

Secure key establishment depends on the arithmetic validity of the public key. To explain the assurance requirements, some terminology needs to be defined. The owner of a static key pair is defined as the entity that is authorized to use the private key that corresponds to the public key; this is independent of whether or not the owner generated the key pair. The recipient of a static public key is defined as the entity that is participating in a key establishment transaction with the owner and obtains the key before or during the current transaction. The owner of an ephemeral public key is the entity that generated the key as part of a key establishment transaction. The recipient of an ephemeral public key is the entity that receives the key during a key establishment transaction with the owner.

Both the owner and a recipient of a candidate public key **shall** have assurance of its arithmetic validity before using it, as specified below. The application performing the key establishment on behalf of the owner and recipient **should** determine whether or not to allow key establishment based upon the method(s) of assurance that was used. Such knowledge may be explicitly provided to the application in some manner, or may be implicitly provided by the operation of the application itself. Prior to obtaining this assurance of arithmetic validity, the owner and recipient of the public key **shall** have assurance of the validity of the domain parameters. The procedures presented for obtaining public key validity assume that the domain parameters have been validated.

5.6.2.1 Owner Assurances of Static Public Key Validity

The owner of a static public key **shall** obtain assurance of its validity in one or more of the following ways:

1. Owner Full Validation - The owner performs a successful full public key validation (see Sections 5.6.2.4 and 5.6.2.5). For example, a key generation routine may perform full public key validation as part of its processing.

2. TTP Full Validation – The owner receives assurance that a trusted third party (trusted by the owner) has performed a successful full public key validation (see Sections 5.6.2.4 and 5.6.2.5).

3. Owner Generation – The owner has generated the public key from the private key (see Section 5.6.1).

4. TTP Generation – The owner has received assurance that a trusted third party (trusted by the owner) has generated the public/private key pair and has provided the key pair to the owner (see Section 5.6.1).

The application performing the key establishment on behalf of the owner **should** determine whether or not to allow key establishment based upon the method(s) of assurance that was used. Such knowledge may be explicitly provided to the application in some manner, or may be implicitly provided by the operation of the application itself. Note that the use of a TTP to generate a key pair for an owner means that the TTP is trusted (by both the owner and any recipient) to not use the owner's private key to masquerade as the owner.

5.6.2.2 Recipient Assurances of Static Public Key Validity

The recipient of a static public key **shall** obtain assurance of its validity in one or more of the following ways:

1. Recipient Full Validation - The recipient performs a successful full public key validation (see Sections 5.6.2.4 and 5.6.2.5).

2. TTP Full Validation – The recipient receives assurance that a trusted third party (trusted by the recipient) has performed a successful full public key validation (see Sections 5.6.2.4 and 5.6.2.5).

3. TTP Generation – The recipient receives assurance that a trusted third party (trusted by the recipient) has generated the public/private key pair in accordance with Section 5.6.1 and has provided the key pair to the owner.

The application performing the key establishment on behalf of the recipient **should** determine whether or not to allow key establishment based upon the method(s) of assurance that was used. Such knowledge may be explicitly provided to the application in some manner, or may be implicitly provided by the operation of the application itself. Note that the use of a TTP to generate a key means that the TTP is trusted (by both the recipient and the owner) to not use the owner's private key to masquerade as the owner.

5.6.2.3 Recipient Assurances of Ephemeral Public Key Validity

The recipient of an ephemeral public key **shall** obtain assurance of its validity in one or more of the following ways:

1. Recipient Full Validation - The recipient performs a successful full public key validation (see Sections 5.6.2.4 and 5.6.2.5).

2. TTP Full Validation – The recipient receives assurance that a trusted third party (trusted by the recipient) has performed a successful full public key validation (see Sections 5.6.2.4 and 5.6.2.5). For example, a trusted processor may only forward an ephemeral public key to the recipient if the public key passes a full public key validation.

3. Recipient ECC Partial Validation - If using an ECC method (only), the recipient performs a successful partial public key validation (see Section 5.6.2.6).

4. TTP ECC Partial Validation – If using an ECC method (only), the recipient receives assurance that a trusted third party (trusted by the recipient) has performed a successful partial public key validation (see Section 5.6.2.6). For example, a trusted processor may only forward an ECC ephemeral public key to the recipient if it passes a partial public key validation.

The application performing the key establishment on behalf of the recipient **should** determine whether or not to allow key establishment based upon the method(s) of assurance that was used. Such knowledge may be explicitly provided to the application in some manner, or may be implicitly provided by the operation of the application itself.

5.6.2.4 FFC Full Public Key Validation Routine

FFC full public key validation refers to the process of checking all the arithmetic properties of a candidate FFC public key to ensure that it has the unique correct representation in the correct subgroup (and therefore is also in the correct multiplicative group) of the finite field specified by the associated FFC domain parameters. FFC full public key validation does not require knowledge of the associated private key and so may be done at any time by anyone. This method **shall** be used with static and ephemeral FFC public keys when assurance of the validity of the keys is obtained by method 1 or method 2 of Sections 5.6.2.1, 5.6.2.2, and 5.6.2.3.

Input:

1. $(p, q, g\{, SEED, pgenCounter\})$: A valid set of FFC domain parameters, and

2. y: A candidate FFC public key.

Process:

1. Verify that $2 \leq y \leq p\text{-}2$.

    (Ensures that the key has the unique correct representation and range in the field.)

2. Verify that $y^q = 1 \pmod p$.

(Ensures that the key has the correct order and is in the correct subgroup.)

Output: If any of the above checks fail, then output an error indicator. Otherwise, output an indication of successful full validation.

5.6.2.5 ECC Full Public Key Validation Routine

ECC full public key validation refers to the process of checking all the arithmetic properties of a candidate ECC public key to ensure that it has the unique correct representation in the correct (additive) subgroup (and therefore is also in the correct EC group) specified by the associated ECC domain parameters. ECC full public key validation does not require knowledge of the associated private key and so may be done at any time by anyone. This method may be used for a static ECC public key, or an ephemeral ECC public key, when assurance of the validity of the key is obtained by method 1 or method 2 of Sections 5.6.2.1, 5.6.2.2, and 5.6.2.3.

Input:
1. $(q, FR, a, b\{, SEED\}, G, n, h)$: A valid set of ECC domain parameters, and
2. $Q=(x_Q, y_Q)$: A candidate ECC public key.

Process:
1. Verify that Q is not the point at infinity O. This can be done by inspection if the point is entered in the standard affine representation.

    (Partial check of the public key for an invalid range in the EC group.)

2. Verify that x_Q and y_Q are integers in the interval $[0, p\text{-}1]$ in the case that q is an odd prime p, or that x_Q and y_Q are bit strings of length m bits in the case that $q = 2^m$.

    (Ensures that each coordinate of the public key has the unique correct representation of an element in the underlying field.)

3. If q is an odd prime p, verify that $(y_Q)^2 \equiv (x_Q)^3 + ax_Q + b \pmod p$.

    If $q = 2^m$, verify that $(y_Q)^2 + x_Q y_Q = (x_Q)^3 + a(x_Q)^2 + b$ in the finite field of size 2^m.

    (Ensures that the public key is on the correct elliptic curve.)

4. Verify that $nQ = O$.

    (Ensures that the public key has the correct order. Along with check 1, ensures that the public key is in the correct range in the correct EC subgroup, that is, it is in the correct EC subgroup and is not the identity element.)

Output: If any of the above checks fail, then output an error indicator. Otherwise, output an indication of successful validation.

5.6.2.6 ECC Partial Public Key Validation Routine

ECC partial public key validation refers to the process of checking some (but not all) of the arithmetic properties of a candidate ECC public key to ensure that it is in the correct group (but not necessarily the correct subgroup) specified by the associated ECC domain parameters. ECC Partial Public Key Validation omits the validation of subgroup membership, and therefore is usually faster than ECC Full Public Key Validation. ECC partial public key validation does not require knowledge of the associated private key and so may be done at any time by anyone. This method may only be used for an ephemeral ECC public key when assurance of the validity of the key is obtained by method 3 or 4 of Section 5.6.2.3.

Input:

1. $(q, FR, a, b\{, SEED\}, G, n, h)$: A valid set of ECC domain parameters, and

2. $Q = (x_Q, y_Q)$: A candidate ECC public key.

Process:

1. Verify that Q is not the point at infinity O. This can be done by inspection if the point is entered in the standard affine representation.

    (Partial check of the public key for an invalid range in the EC group.)

2. Verify that x_Q and y_Q are integers in the interval $[0, p\text{-}1]$ in the case that q is an odd prime p, or that x_Q and y_Q are bit strings of length m bits in the case that $q = 2^m$.

    (Ensures that each coordinate of the public key has the unique correct representation of an element in the underlying field.)

3. If q is an odd prime p, verify that $(y_Q)^2 \equiv (x_Q)^3 + ax_Q + b \pmod{p}$.

    If $q = 2^m$, verify that $(y_Q)^2 + x_Q\, y_Q = (x_Q)^3 + a(x_Q)^2 + b$ in the finite field of size 2^m.

    (Ensures that the public key is on the correct elliptic curve.)

    (Note: Since its order is not verified, there is no check that the public key is in the correct EC subgroup.)

Output: If any of the above checks fail, then output an error indicator. Otherwise, output an indication of validation success.

5.6.3 Assurances of the Possession of a Static Private Key

The security of key agreement schemes that use static key pairs depends on limiting knowledge of the static private keys to those who have been authorized to use them (i.e., their respective owners). In addition to preventing unauthorized entities from gaining access to private keys, it is also important to obtain assurance that authorized users do have access to their correct static private keys.

Assurance of possession requirements for the owner of a static private key are specified in Section 5.6.3.1. Assurance of possession requirements for recipients of a static public key are specified in Section 5.6.3.2.

When assurance of possession of a static private key is obtained, the assurance of the validity of the associated public key **shall** be obtained either prior to or concurrently with obtaining assurance of possession. Note that as time passes, an owner may lose possession of the associated private key, either by choice or due to an error; for this reason, current assurance of possession can be of more value for some applications. See Section 5.6.3.2.2 and Section 8.1 for ways to obtain more current assurance of possession.

5.6.3.1 Owner Assurances of Possession of a Static Private Key

The owner of a static public key **shall** have assurance that the owner actually possesses the correct associated private key in one or more of the following ways:

1. Owner Receives Assurance via Explicit Key Confirmation – The owner employs the static key pair to successfully engage another party in a key agreement transaction incorporating explicit key confirmation. The key confirmation **shall** be performed with the owner as key confirmation recipient in order to obtain assurance that the private key functions correctly. See Section 8 for further explanation.

2. Owner Receives Assurance via Use of an Encrypted Certificate - The owner uses the static private key while engaging in a key agreement transaction with a Certificate Authority (trusted by the owner), providing the CA with the corresponding static public key. As part of this transaction, the CA generates a certificate containing the owner's static public key and encrypts the certificate using a symmetric key derived from the shared secret they have (allegedly) established. Only the encrypted form of the certificate is provided to the owner. By successfully decrypting the certificate, the owner obtains assurance of possession of the correct private key (at the time of the key agreement transaction).

3. Owner Receives Assurance via Key Regeneration – The owner regenerates a public key from the static private key and verifies that the regenerated public key is equal to the original static public key. Note that this method may be useful if the static private key has been generated by a party other than the owner or as an integrity check on a key pair that has been stored for a long period of time.

4. Owner Receives Assurance via Trusted Provision - A trusted party (trusted by the owner) provides the static private key and static public key to the owner using a trusted distribution method. Reliance upon this method assumes (1) that the trusted party will provide a private key that is consistent with the public key and (2) that the trusted party will not use the private key to masquerade as the owner.

5. Owner Receives Assurance via Key Generation - The act of generating a key pair, with the public key being computed from the private key, is a way for the owner to obtain assurance of possession of the correct private key. This method allows an owner who

protects his/her own keys to have assurance of possession without additional computation. Note that this method may not detect algorithm implementation errors, hardware errors, random bit flips, etc. Further assurance may be obtained through the use of one or more of the above methods.

The owner of a static public key (or agents trusted to act on the owner's behalf) **should** determine that the method used for obtaining assurance of the owner's possession of the correct static private key is sufficient and appropriate to meet the security requirements of the owner's intended application(s).

5.6.3.2 Recipient Assurance of Owner's Possession of a Static Private Key

At the time of binding an identifier to the owner's static public key, the binding authority **shall** obtain assurance that the owner is in possession of the correct static private key. This assurance **shall** either be obtained using one of the methods specified in Section 5.6.3.2.2 or by using an Approved alternative.

Recipients other than binding authorities shall obtain this assurance – either through a trusted third party (see Section 5.6.3.2.1) or directly – before using the derived keying material for purposes beyond those required during the key agreement transaction itself. If the recipient chooses to obtain this assurance directly, then to comply with this Recommendation the parties **shall** use one of the methods specified in Section 5.6.3.2.2.

5.6.3.2.1   Recipient Obtains Assurance through a Trusted Third Party

The recipient of a static public key may receive assurance that its owner is in possession of the correct static private key from a trusted third party, either before or during a key agreement transaction that makes use of that static public key. The methods used by a third party trusted by the recipient to obtain that assurance are beyond the scope of this Recommendation (see however, Section 8.1.5.1.1.2 of SP 800-57 [7]). The recipient of a static public key (or agents trusted to act on behalf of the recipient) **should** know the method(s) used by the third party, in order to determine that the assurance obtained on behalf of the recipient is sufficient and appropriate to meet the security requirements of the recipient's intended application(s).

5.6.3.2.2   Recipient Obtains Assurance Directly from the Claimed Owner

When two parties engage in a key agreement transaction, there is (at least) an implicit claim of ownership made whenever a static public key is provided on behalf of a particular party. That party is considered to be a *claimed* owner of the corresponding static key pair – as opposed to being a *true* owner – until adequate assurance can be provided that the party is actually the one authorized to use the static private key.

The recipient of a static public key can directly obtain assurance of the claimed owner's current possession of the corresponding private key by successfully completing a key agreement transaction that explicitly incorporates key confirmation, with the claimed owner serving as the key confirmation provider (see Section 8). Note that the recipient of the static public key in question is also the key confirmation recipient. When assurance of possession is obtained through key confirmation performed in compliance with this Recommendation, the underlying key agreement scheme used **shall** be one of the following, and the recipient seeking assurance **shall** serve as the key agreement initiator:

- dhHybridOneFlow or (Cofactor) One-Pass Unified Model,

- MQV1 or One-Pass MQV,

- dhOneFlow or (Cofactor) One-Pass Diffie-Hellman.

(See Sections 6 and 8 for details.) The recipient of a static public key (or agents trusted to act on the recipient's behalf) **shall** determine that the key agreement scheme employed to obtain assurance of possession in this manner is sufficient and appropriate to meet the security requirements of the recipient's intended application(s).

In each of the permitted scenarios, the key confirmation recipient contributes (at least) an ephemeral public key that must be arithmetically combined with the static private key claimed by the key confirmation provider during the provider's computation of the shared secret. Successful key confirmation (performed in the context described here) demonstrates that the correct static private key has been used in the key confirmation provider's calculations, and thus also provides assurance that the claimed owner is the true owner (see Section 8.1).

Key confirmation may be requested by the recipient even when the recipient has obtained independent assurance that the claimed owner of a static public key is indeed its true owner. This is appropriate in situations where the recipient desires assurance that the owner is currently in possession of the correct static private key (and that the owner is currently able to use it correctly), or in situations where there is no access to a trusted party who can provide assurance of the owner's (previous) demonstration of private key possession.

Note that the recommendation that assurance of possession be obtained before using derived keying material for purposes *beyond* those of the key agreement transaction itself does not prohibit the parties to a key agreement transaction from using derived keying material *during* the transaction, for purposes required by the key agreement scheme. For example, in a transaction involving a key agreement scheme that incorporates key confirmation, the parties establish a (purportedly) shared secret, derive keying material, and — as part of that same transaction — use a portion of the derived keying material as the *MacKey* in their key confirmation computations.

5.6.4 Key Pair Management

5.6.4.1 Common Requirements on Static and Ephemeral Key Pairs

The following are common requirements on static and ephemeral key pairs (see the Recommendation for Key Management [7]):

1. A public/private key pair **shall** be correctly associated with its corresponding specific set of domain parameters. Each key pair **shall not** be used with more than one set of domain parameters.

2. Each DLC private key **shall** be unpredictable and created using an Approved key generation method as specified in Section 5.6.1.

3. Private keys **shall** be protected from unauthorized access, disclosure, modification and substitution.

4. Public keys **shall** be protected from unauthorized modification and substitution. This is often accomplished by using public key certificates that have been signed by a Certification Authority (CA).

5.6.4.2 Specific Requirements on Static Key Pairs

The specific requirements for static key pairs are as follows:

1. A recipient of a static public key **shall** be assured of the data integrity and correct association of (a) the public key, (b) the set of domain parameters for that key, and (c) the identifier of the entity that owns the key pair (that is, the party with whom the recipient intends to establish a key). This assurance is often provided by verifying a public-key certificate that was signed by a trusted third party (for example, a CA), but may be provided by direct distribution of the keying material from the owner, provided that the recipient trusts the owner to do this.

2. A static key pair may be used in more than one key establishment scheme. However, one static public/private key pair **shall not** be used for different purposes (for example, a digital signature key pair is not to be used for key establishment or vice versa) with the following possible exception: when requesting the (initial) certificate for a public static key establishment key, the key establishment private key associated with the public key may be used to sign the certificate request. See SP 800-57, Part 1 on Key Usage for further information.

3. An owner and a recipient of a static public key **shall** have assurance of the validity of the public key. This assurance may be provided, for example, through the use of a public key certificate if the CA obtains sufficient assurance of public key validity as part of its certification process. See Section 5.6.2. The application performing the key establishment on behalf of the recipient **should** determine whether or not to allow key establishment based upon the method(s) of assurance that was used. Such knowledge may be explicitly provided to the application in some manner, or may be implicitly provided by the operation of the application itself.

4. An owner and a recipient of a static public key **shall** have assurance of the owner's possession of the associated private key (see Section 5.6.3). The owner **shall** know the method used to obtain assurance of possession of the owner's private key. The recipient **shall** know the method used to provide assurance to the recipient of the owner's possession of the private key. This assurance may be provided, for example, through the use of a public key certificate if the CA obtains sufficient assurance of possession as part of its certification process.

5.6.4.3 Specific Requirements on Ephemeral Key Pairs

The specific requirements on ephemeral key pairs are as follows:

1. An ephemeral private key **shall** be used in exactly one key establishment transaction, with one exception: an ephemeral private key may be used in multiple DLC Key Transport transactions that are transporting identical secret keying material simultaneously (or within a short period of time; see Section 7). After its use, an ephemeral private key **shall** be zeroized.

2. An ephemeral key pair **should** be generated as close to its time of use as possible. Ideally, an ephemeral key pair is generated just before the ephemeral public key is transmitted.

3. A recipient of an ephemeral public key **shall** have assurance of the validity of the public key (see Section 5.6.2). The application performing the key establishment on behalf of the recipient **should** determine whether or not to allow key establishment based upon the method(s) of assurance that was used. Such knowledge may be explicitly provided to the application in some manner, or may be implicitly provided by the operation of the application itself.

5.7 DLC Primitives

A primitive is a relatively simple operation that is defined to facilitate implementation in hardware or in a software subroutine. Each key establishment scheme **shall** use exactly one DLC primitive. Each scheme in Section 6 **shall** use an appropriate primitive from the following list:

1. The FFC DH primitive (Section 5.7.1.1 of this Recommendation): This primitive **shall** be used by the dhHybrid1, dhEphem, dhHybridOneFlow, dhOneFlow and dhStatic schemes, which are based on finite field cryptography and the Diffie-Hellman algorithm.

2. The ECC CDH primitive (Section 5.7.1.2 of this Recommendation and called the Modified Diffie-Hellman primitive in ANS X9.63): This primitive **shall** be used by the Full Unified Model, Ephemeral Unified Model, One-Pass Unified Model, One-Pass Diffie-Hellman and Static Unified Model schemes, which are based on elliptic curve cryptography and the Diffie-Hellman algorithm.

3. The FFC MQV primitive (Section 5.7.2.1 of this Recommendation): This primitive **shall** be used by the MQV2 and MQV1 schemes, which are based on finite field cryptography and the MQV algorithm.

4. The ECC MQV primitive (Section 5.7.2.2 of this Recommendation): This primitive **shall** be used by the Full MQV and One-Pass MQV schemes, which are based on elliptic curve cryptography and the MQV algorithm.

The shared secret output from these primitives **shall** be used as input to a key derivation function (see Section 5.8).

5.7.1 Diffie-Hellman Primitives

5.7.1.1 Finite Field Cryptography Diffie-Hellman (FFC DH) Primitive

The shared secret Z is computed using the domain parameters (p, q, $g\{$, $SEED$, $pgenCounter\}$), the other party's public key and one's own private key. This primitive is used in Section 6 by the dhHybrid1, dhEphem, dhHybridOneFlow, dhOneFlow and dhStatic schemes. Assume that the party performing the computation is party A, and the other party is party B. Note that party A could be either the initiator U or the responder V.

Input:

1. (p, q, $g\{$, $SEED$, $pgenCounter\}$): Domain parameters,

2. x_A : One's own private key, and

3. y_B : The other party's public key.

Process:

1. $Z = y_B^{x_A} \bmod p$

2. If $Z=1$, output an error indicator.

3. Else, output Z.

Output: The shared secret Z or an error indicator.

5.7.1.2 Elliptic Curve Cryptography Cofactor Diffie-Hellman (ECC CDH) Primitive

The shared secret Z is computed using the domain parameters (q, FR, a, $b\{$, $SEED\}$, G, n, h), the other party's public key, and one's own private key. This primitive is used in Section 6 by the Full Unified Model, Ephemeral Unified Model, One-Pass Unified Model, One-Pass Diffie-Hellman and Static Unified Model schemes. Assume that the party performing the computation is party A, and the other party is party B. Note that party A could be either the initiator U or the responder V.

Input:

1. (q, FR, a, $b\{$, $SEED\}$, G, n, h): Domain parameters,

2. d_A : One's own private key, and

3. Q_B : The other party's public key.

Process:

1. Compute the point $P = hd_AQ_B$.

2. If $P = O$, output an error indicator.

3. $Z = x_P$ where x_P is the x-coordinate of P.

Output: The shared secret Z or an error indicator.

5.7.2 MQV Primitives

5.7.2.1 Finite Field Cryptography MQV (FFC MQV) Primitive

The shared secret Z is computed using the domain parameters $(p, q, g\{, SEED, pgenCounter\})$, the other party's public keys and one's own public and private keys. Assume that the party performing the computation is party A, and the other party is party B. Note that party A could be either the initiator U or the responder V.

Input:

1. $(p, q, g\{, SEED, pgenCounter\})$: Domain parameters,

2. x_A : One's own static private key,

3. y_B : The other party's static public key,

4. r_A : One's own second private key,[3]

5. t_A : One's own second public key, and

6. t_B : The other party's second public key.

Process:

1. $w = \lceil |q|/2 \rceil$.

2. $T_A = (t_A \bmod 2^w) + 2^w$.

3. $S_A = (r_A + T_A x_A) \bmod q$.

4. $T_B = (t_B \bmod 2^w) + 2^w$.

5. $Z = ((t_B (y_B^{T_B}))^{S_A}) \bmod p$.

6. If $Z = 1$, output an error indicator. Else, output Z.

Output: The shared secret Z or an error indicator.

5.7.2.1.1 MQV2 Form of the FFC MQV Primitive

This form of invoking the FFC MQV primitive is used in Section 6.1.1.3 by the MQV2 scheme. In this form, each party uses both a static key pair and an ephemeral key pair. Assume that the

---

[3] In the FFC MQV primitive, a second key may be either ephemeral or static, depending on which form is being used, see Sections 5.7.2.1.1 and 5.7.2.1.2.

party performing the computation is party A, and the other party is party B. Note that party A could be either the initiator U or the responder V.

In this form, one's own second private and public keys (input 4 and 5 in Section 5.7.2.1) are one's own ephemeral private and public keys (r_A and t_A), and the other party's second public key (input 6 in Section 5.7.2.1) is the other party's ephemeral public key (t_B).

5.7.2.1.2   MQV1 Form of the FFC MQV Primitive

This form of invoking the FFC MQV primitive is used in Section 6.2.1.3 by the MQV1 scheme. In this form, the initiator uses a static key pair and an ephemeral key pair, but the responder uses only a static key pair. One-Pass MQV is done using the MQV primitive by using the responder's static key pair as the responder's second key pair (as the responder has no ephemeral key pair).

The initiator uses the responder's static public key for the responder's second public key; that is, when the initiator uses the algorithm in Section 5.7.2.1, input 6 becomes the other party's static public key (y_B).

The responder uses his/her static private key for his second private key; that is, when the responder uses the algorithm in Section 5.7.2.1, input 4 becomes the responder's static private key x_A, and input 5 becomes the responder's static public key (y_A).

5.7.2.2 ECC MQV Associate Value Function

The associate value function is used by the ECC MQV family of key agreement schemes to compute an integer that is associated with an elliptic curve point. This Recommendation defines avf(Q) to be the associate value function of a public key Q using the domain parameters (q, FR, a, $b\{$, SEED$\}$, G, n, h).

Input:

1. (q, FR, a, $b\{$, SEED$\}$, G, n, h): Domain parameters, and

2. Q: A public key (that is, a point on the subgroup not equal to the point at infinity).

Process:

1. Convert x_Q to an integer xqi using the convention specified in Appendix C.3.

2. Calculate

    $xqm = xqi \bmod 2^{\lceil f/2 \rceil}$ (where $f = \lceil \log_2 n \rceil$).

3. Calculate the associate value function

    avf(Q) = $xqm + 2^{\lceil f/2 \rceil}$. (See footnote[4]).

---

[4] Note that avf(Q) can be computed using only bit operations.

Output: avf(Q), the associate value of Q.

5.7.2.3 Elliptic Curve Cryptography MQV (ECC MQV) Primitive

The ECC MQV primitive is computed using the domain parameters (q, FR, a, $b\{$, $SEED\}$, G, n, h), the other party's public keys, and one's own public and private keys. The ECC version of MQV uses the cofactor h in its calculations. Assume that the party performing the computation is party A, and the other party is party B. Note that party A could be either the scheme initiator U or the scheme responder V.

Input:

1. (q, FR, a, $b\{$, $SEED\}$, G, n, h): Domain parameters,

2. $d_{s,A}$: One's own static private key,

3. $Q_{s,B}$: The other party's static public key,

4. $d_{e,A}$: One's own second private key,[5]

5. $Q_{e,A}$: One's own second public key, and

6. $Q_{e,B}$: The other party's second public key.

Process:

1. $implicitsig_A = (d_{e,A} + \mathrm{avf}(Q_{e,A})d_{s,A}) \bmod n$.

2. $P = h(implicitsig_A)(Q_{e,B} + \mathrm{avf}(Q_{e,B})Q_{s,B})$.

3. If $P = O$, output an error indicator.

4. $Z = x_P$, where x_P is the x-coordinate of P.

Output: The shared secret Z or an error indicator.

5.7.2.3.1   Full MQV Form of the ECC MQV Primitive

This form of invoking the ECC MQV primitive is used in Section 6.1.1.4 by the Full MQV scheme. In this form, each party has both a static key pair and an ephemeral key pair. Assume that the party performing the computation is party A, and the other party is party B. Note that party A could be either the initiator U or the responder V.

In this form, one's own second private and public keys (input 4 and 5 in Section 5.7.2.3) are one's own ephemeral private and public keys ($d_{e,A}$ and $Q_{e,A}$), and the other party's second public key (input 6 in Section 5.7.2.3) is the other party's ephemeral public key ($Q_{e,B}$).

---

[5] In the ECC MQV primitive, a second key may be either ephemeral or static, depending on which form is being used, see Sections 5.7.2.3.1 and 5.7.2.3.2.

5.7.2.3.2 One-Pass Form of the ECC MQV Primitive

This form of invoking the ECC MQV primitive is used in Section 6.2.1.4 by the One-Pass MQV scheme. In this form, the initiator has a static key pair and an ephemeral key pair, but the responder has only a static key pair. One-Pass MQV is done using the MQV primitive with the responder's static key pair as the responder's second key pair (as the responder has no ephemeral keys).

The initiator uses the responder's static public key as the responder's second public key. When the initiator uses the algorithm in Section 5.7.2.3, input 6 becomes the other party's static public key ($Q_{s,B}$).

The responder uses his static private key as his second private key. When the responder uses the algorithm in Section 5.7.2.3, input 4 becomes the responder's static private key $d_{s,A}$, and input 5 becomes the responder's static public key ($Q_{s,A}$).

5.8 Key Derivation Functions for Key Agreement Schemes

An Approved key derivation function (KDF) **shall** be used to derive secret keying material from a shared secret. The output from a KDF **shall** only be used for secret keying material, such as a symmetric key used for data encryption or message integrity, a secret initialization vector, or a master key that will be used to generate other keys (possibly using a different process). Non-secret keying material (such as a non-secret initialization vector) **shall not** be generated using the shared secret.

Each call to the KDF requires a freshly computed shared secret, and this shared secret **shall** be zeroized immediately following its use. The derived secret keying material **shall** be computed in its entirety before outputting any portion of it. In schemes using only static keys, the freshly computed shared secret may be the same as the previous shared secret. In these cases, the initiator supplied nonce (*Nonce$_U$*, see Section 6.3) used in the scheme will vary so the same keying material is not regenerated.

The derived secret keying material may be parsed into one or more keys or other secret cryptographic keying material (for example, secret initialization vectors). If Key Confirmation (KC) or implementation validation testing are to be performed as specified in Section 8 or Section 5.2.3, respectively, then the MAC key **shall** be formed from the first bits of the KDF output and zeroized after its use (i.e., the MAC key **shall not** be used for purposes other than key confirmation or implementation validation testing).

This section specifies two Approved KDFs for use in key establishment. The Approved methods are provided in Section 5.8.1 and 5.8.2. Other key derivation methods may be temporarily allowed for backward compatibility. These other allowable methods and any restrictions on their use will be specified in FIPS 140-2 Annex D. Any hash function used in a KDF **shall** be Approved (see Section 5.1) and **shall** also meet the selection requirements specified herein (see Section 5.5.1).

5.8.1 Concatenation Key Derivation Function (Approved Alternative 1)

This section specifies an Approved key derivation function, based on concatenation.

The Concatenation KDF is as follows:

Function call: kdf (Z, *OtherInput*),

> where *OtherInput* is *keydatalen* and *OtherInfo*.

Fixed Values (implementation dependent):

1. *hashlen*: an integer that indicates the length (in bits) of the output of the hash function used to derive blocks of secret keying material.

2. *max_hash_inputlen*: an integer that indicates the maximum length (in bits) of the bit string(s) input to the hash function.

Auxiliary Function:

1. H: an Approved hash function.

Input:

1. Z: a byte string that is the shared secret.

2. *keydatalen*: An integer that indicates the length (in bits) of the secret keying material to be generated; *keydatalen* **shall** be less than or equal to $hashlen \times (2^{32} - 1)$.

3. *OtherInfo*: A bit string equal to the following concatenation:

   > *AlgorithmID* || *PartyUInfo* || *PartyVInfo* {|| *SuppPubInfo* }{|| *SuppPrivInfo* }

   where the subfields are defined as follows:

   3.1 *AlgorithmID*: A bit string that indicates how the derived keying material will be parsed and for which algorithm(s) the derived secret keying material will be used. For example, *AlgorithmID* might indicate that bits 1-80 are to be used as an 80-bit HMAC key and that bits 81-208 are to be used as a 128-bit AES key.

   3.2 *PartyUInfo*: A bit string containing public information that is required by the application using this KDF to be contributed by party U to the key derivation process. At a minimum, *PartyUInfo* **shall** include ID_U, the identifier of party U. See the notes below.

   3.3 *PartyVInfo*: A bit string containing public information that is required by the application using this KDF to be contributed by party V to the key derivation process. At a minimum, *PartyVInfo* **shall** include ID_V, the identifier of party V. See the notes below.

   3.4 (Optional) *SuppPubInfo*: A bit string containing additional, mutually-known public information.

3.5   (Optional) *SuppPrivInfo*: A bit string containing additional, mutually-known private information (for example, a shared secret symmetric key that has been communicated through a separate channel).

Each of the three subfields *AlgorithmID*, *PartyUInfo*, and *PartyVInfo* **shall** be the concatenation of an application-specific, fixed-length sequence of substrings of information. Each substring representing a separate unit of information **shall** have one of these two formats: Either it is a fixed-length bit string, or it has the form *Datalen* || *Data*, where *Data* is a variable-length string of zero or more bytes, and *Datalen* is a fixed-length, big-endian counter that indicates the length (in bytes) of *Data*. (In this variable-length format, a null string of data **shall** be represented by using *Datalen* to indicate that *Data* has length zero.) An application using this KDF **shall** specify the ordering and number of the separate information substrings used in each of the subfields *AlgorithmID*, *PartyUInfo*, and *PartyVInfo*, and **shall** also specify which of the two formats (fixed-length or variable-length) is used for each substring. The application **shall** specify the lengths for all fixed-length quantities, including the *Datalen* counters.

The subfields *SuppPrivInfo* and *SuppPubInfo* (when allowed by the application) **shall** be formed by the concatenation of an application-specific, fixed-length sequence of substrings of additional information that may be used in key derivation upon mutual agreement of parties *U* and *V*. Each substring representing a separate unit of information **shall** be of the form *Datalen* || *Data*, where *Data* is a variable-length string of zero or more (eight-bit) bytes and *Datalen* is a fixed-length, big-endian counter that indicates the length (in bytes) of *Data*. The information substrings that parties *U* and *V* choose not to contribute are set equal to *Null*, and are represented in this variable-length format by setting *Datalen* equal to zero. If an application allows the use of the *OtherInfo* subfield *SuppPrivInfo* and/or the subfield *SuppPubInfo*, then the application **shall** specify the ordering and the number of additional information substrings that may be used in the allowed subfield(s) and **shall** specify the fixed-length of the *Datalen* counters.

Process:

1. *reps* = $\lceil$ *keydatalen* / *hashlen* $\rceil$.

2. If *reps* > $(2^{32} - 1)$, then ABORT: output an error indicator and stop.

3. Initialize a 32-bit, big-endian bit string *counter* as 00000001_{16}.

4. If *counter* || *Z* || *OtherInfo* is more than *max_hash_inputlen* bits long, then ABORT: output an error indicator and stop.

5. For *i* = 1 to *reps* by 1, do the following:

    5.1   Compute $Hash_i$ = H(*counter* || *Z* || *OtherInfo*).

    5.2   Increment *counter* (modulo 2^{32}), treating it as an unsigned 32-bit integer.

47

6. Let *Hhash* be set to *Hash*$_{reps}$ if (*keydatalen* / *hashlen*) is an integer; otherwise, let *Hhash* be set to the (*keydatalen* mod *hashlen*) leftmost bits of *Hash*$_{reps}$.

7. Set *DerivedKeyingMaterial* = *Hash*$_1$ || *Hash*$_2$ || … || *Hash*$_{reps-1}$ || *Hhash*.

Output:

The bit string *DerivedKeyingMaterial* of length *keydatalen* bits (or an error indicator). Any scheme attempting to call this key derivation function with *keydatalen* greater than or equal to *hashlen* × (2^{32} −1) **shall** output an error indicator and stop without outputting *DerivedKeyingMaterial*. Any call to the key derivation function involving an attempt to hash a bit string that is greater than *max_hash_inputlen* bits long **shall** cause the KDF to output an error indicator and stop without outputting *DerivedKeyingMaterial*.

Notes:

1. *ID$_U$* and *ID$_V$* **shall** be represented in *OtherInfo* as separate units of information, using either the fixed-length format or the variable-length format described above – according to the requirements of the application using this KDF. The rationale for including the identifiers in the KDF input is provided in Appendix B.

2. Party *U* **shall** be the initiator, and party *V* **shall** be the responder, as assigned by the protocol employing the key agreement scheme used to determine the shared secret *Z*.

5.8.2 ASN.1 Key Derivation Function (Approved Alternative 2)

This section specifies an Approved key derivation function utilizing ASN.1 DER encoding of *OtherInfo*. In all other respects, it is the same as the key derivation function specified in Section 5.8.1.

The ASN.1 KDF is as follows:

Function call: kdf (*Z, OtherInput*)

where *OtherInput* is *keydatalen* and *OtherInfo*.

Fixed Values (implementation dependent):

1. *hashlen*: an integer that indicates the length (in bits) of the output of the hash function used to derive blocks of secret keying material.

2. *max_hash_inputlen*: an integer that indicates the maximum length (in bits) of the bit string(s) input to the hash function.

Auxiliary Function:

1. H: an Approved hash function.

Input:

1. *Z*: a byte string that is the shared secret.

2. *keydatalen*: An integer that indicates the length (in bits) of the secret keying material to be generated; *keydatalen* **shall** be less than or equal to *hashlen* $\times$ ($2^{32}-1$).

3. *OtherInfo*: A bit string specified in ASN.1 DER encoding, which consists of the following information:

   3.1 *AlgorithmID*: A bit string that indicates how the derived keying material will be parsed and for which algorithm(s) the derived secret keying material will be used. For example, *AlgorithmID* might indicate that bits 1-80 are to be used as an 80-bit HMAC key and that bits 81-208 are to be used as a 128-bit AES key.

   3.2 *PartyUInfo*: A bit string containing public information that is required by the application using this KDF to be contributed by party *U* to the key derivation process. At a minimum, *PartyUInfo* **shall** include ID_U, the identifier of party *U*. See the notes below.

   3.3 *PartyVInfo*: A bit string containing public information that is required by the application using this KDF to be contributed by party *V* to the key derivation process. At a minimum, *PartyVInfo* **shall** include ID_V, the identifier of party V. See the notes below.

   3.4 (Optional) *SuppPubInfo*: A bit string containing additional, mutually-known public information.

   3.5 (Optional) *SuppPrivInfo*: A bit string containing additional, mutually-known private information (for example, a shared secret symmetric key that has been communicated through a separate channel).

Process:

1. $reps = \lceil keydatalen / hashlen \rceil$.

2. If $reps > (2^{32}-1)$, then ABORT: output an error indicator and stop.

3. Initialize a 32-bit, big-endian bit string *counter* as 00000001_{16}.

4. If *counter* $\| Z \|$ *OtherInfo* is more than *max_hash_inputlen* bits long, then ABORT: output an error indicator and stop.

5. For $i = 1$ to *reps* by 1, do the following:

   5.1 Compute $Hash_i = H(counter \| Z \| OtherInfo)$.

   5.2 Increment *counter* (modulo 2^{32}), treating it as an unsigned 32-bit integer.

6. Let *Hhash* be set to $Hash_{reps}$ if (*keydatalen* / *hashlen*) is an integer; otherwise, let *Hhash* be set to the (*keydatalen* mod *hashlen*) leftmost bits of $Hash_{reps}$.

7. Set *DerivedKeyingMaterial* = $Hash_1 \| Hash_2 \| ... \| Hash_{reps-1} \| Hhash$.

Output:

The *DerivedKeyingMaterial* as a bit string of length *keydatalen* bits (or an error indicator). The ASN.1 KDF produces secret keying material that is at most *hashlen* $\times$ $(2^{32}$ $-1)$ bits in length. Any call to this key derivation function using a *keydatalen* value that is greater than *hashlen* $\times$ $(2^{32}-1)$ **shall** cause the KDF to output an error indicator and stop without outputting *DerivedKeyingMaterial*. Any call to the key derivation function involving an attempt to hash a bit string that is greater than *max_hash_inputlen* bits long **shall** cause the KDF to output an error indicator and stop without outputting *DerivedKeyingMaterial*.

Notes:

1. *ID$_U$* and *ID$_V$* **shall** be represented in *OtherInfo* as separate units of information. The rationale for including the identifiers in the KDF input is provided in Appendix B.

2. Party U **shall** be the initiator, and party V **shall** be the responder, as assigned by the protocol employing the key agreement scheme used to determine the shared secret Z.

6.   Key Agreement

This Recommendation provides three **categories** of key agreement schemes (see Table 3). The classification of the categories is based on the number of ephemeral keys used by the two parties to the key agreement process, parties U and V. In category C(i), parties U and V have a total of i ephemeral key pairs. The first category, C(2), consists of schemes requiring the generation of ephemeral key pairs by both parties; a C(2) scheme is suitable for an interactive key establishment protocol. The second category, C(1), consists of schemes requiring the generation of an ephemeral key pair by only one party; a C(1) scheme is suitable for a store and forward scenario, but may also be used in an interactive key establishment protocol. The third category, C(0), consists of schemes that do not use ephemeral keys.

Key confirmation may be added to many of these schemes to provide assurance that the participants share the same keying material; see Section 8 for details on key confirmation. Each party **should** have such assurance. Although other methods are often used to provide this assurance, this Recommendation makes no statement as to the adequacy of these other methods.

Table 3: Key Agreement Scheme Categories

Category	Comment
C(2): Two ephemeral key pairs	Each party generates an ephemeral key pair.
C(1): One ephemeral key pair	Only the initiator generates an ephemeral key pair.
C(0): Zero ephemeral key pairs	No ephemeral keys are used.

Each category is comprised of one or more subcategories that are classified by the use of static keys by the parties (see Table 4). In subcategory C(i, j), parties U and V have a total of i ephemeral key pairs and j static key pairs.

Table 4: Key Agreement Scheme Subcategories

Category	Subcategory
C(2): Two ephemeral key pairs	C(2, 2): Each party generates an ephemeral key pair and has a static key pair.
	C(2, 0): Each party generates an ephemeral key pair; no static key pairs are used.
C(1): One ephemeral key pair	C(1, 2): The initiator generates an ephemeral key pair and has a static key pair; the responder has only a static key pair.
	C(1, 1): The initiator generates an ephemeral key pair, but has no static key pair; the responder has only a static key pair.
C(0): Zero ephemeral key pairs	C(0, 2): Each party has only a static key pair.

The schemes may be further classified by whether they use finite field cryptography (FFC) or elliptic curve cryptography (ECC). A scheme may use either Diffie-Hellman or MQV primitives (see Section 5.7). Thus, for example, C(2, 2, FFC DH) completely classifies the dhHybrid1 scheme of Section 6.1.1.1 as a scheme with two ephemeral keys and two static keys that uses finite field cryptography and a Diffie-Hellman primitive (see Table 5).

Table 5: Key Agreement Schemes

Category	Subcategory	Primitive	Scheme	Full Classification
C(2)	C(2, 2)	FFC DH	dhHybrid1	C(2, 2, FFC DH)
C(2)	C(2, 2)	ECC CDH	(Cofactor) Full Unified Model	C(2, 2, ECC CDH)
C(2)	C(2, 2)	FFC MQV	MQV2	C(2, 2, FFC MQV)
C(2)	C(2, 2)	ECC MQV	Full MQV	C(2, 2, ECC MQV)
C(2)	C(2, 0)	FFC DH	dhEphem	C(2, 0, FFC DH)

Category	Subcategory	Primitive	Scheme	Full Classification
C(2)	C(2, 0)	ECC CDH	(Cofactor) Ephemeral Unified Model	C(2, 0, ECC CDH)
C(1)	C(1, 2)	FFC DH	dhHybridOneFlow	C(1, 2, FFC DH)
C(1)	C(1, 2)	ECC CDH	(Cofactor) One-Pass Unified Model	C(1, 2, ECC CDH)
C(1)	C(1, 2)	FFC MQV	MQV1	C(1, 2, FFC MQV)
C(1)	C(1, 2)	ECC MQV	One-Pass MQV	C(1, 2, ECC MQV)
C(1)	C(1, 1)	FFC DH	dhOneFlow	C(1, 1, FFC DH)
C(1)	C(1, 1)	ECC CDH	(Cofactor) One-Pass Diffie-Hellman	C(1, 1, ECC CDH)
C(0)	C(0, 2)	FFC DH	dhStatic	C(0, 2, FFC DH)
C(0)	C(0, 2)	ECC CDH	Cofactor Static Unified Model	C(0, 2, ECC CDH)

Each party in a key agreement process **shall** use the same set of valid domain parameters. These parameters **shall** be established and validated prior to the initiation of the key agreement process. See Section 5.5 for a discussion of domain parameters.

Party U **shall** have an identifier ID_U. If Party U owns a static key pair that is used in a given key agreement transaction, then ID_U **shall** be the identifier that is bound to that key pair. If Party U does not contribute a static public key as part of a given key agreement transaction, then ID_U **shall** be a non-null identifier selected in accordance with the protocol utilizing the scheme. Similar rules apply for the selection of Party V's identifier, ID_V.

A general flow diagram is provided for each subcategory of schemes. The dotted-line arrows represent the distribution of static public keys that may be distributed by the parties themselves or by a third party, such as a Certification Authority (CA). The solid-line arrows represent the distribution of ephemeral public keys or nonces that occur during the key agreement or key confirmation process. Note that the flow diagrams in this Recommendation omit explicit mention of various validation checks that are required. The flow diagrams and descriptions in this Recommendation assume a successful completion of the key establishment process.

Rationale for selecting schemes for each subcategory, C(i, j), is included. These rationale sections will provide the user or developer with additional information to help make a choice as to which key establishment scheme to use. The rationale includes discussions of the security properties for the schemes. In general, the security properties for each scheme within a subcategory are the same; when this is not the case, the exceptions are identified. See Section 6.1.1.5 specifically. These rationale sections do not contain an in-depth discussion of all possible security properties of all schemes. For further discussion, see ANS X9.42 and ANS X9.63. Note that the specific security properties achieved depend on whether a static key is used, whether an ephemeral key is used, the specific method of calculating the shared secret, and the key confirmation method used, if any.

It is important that a scheme not be chosen based solely on the number of security properties it possesses. Rather, a scheme should be selected based on how well the scheme fulfills the system requirements. For instance, in a bandwidth-constrained system, a scheme with fewer passes per exchange might be preferable to a scheme with more passes and more security properties.

It is also important to understand that a scheme may be a component of a protocol, which in turn provides additional security properties not provided by the scheme when considered by itself. Note that protocols, per se, are not specified in this Recommendation.

6.1   Schemes Using Two Ephemeral Key Pairs, C(2)

In this category, each party generates an ephemeral key pair and sends the ephemeral public key to the other party. This category consists of two subcategories that are determined by the use of static keys by the parties. In the first subcategory, each party has both static and ephemeral keys (see Section 6.1.1), while in the second subcategory, each party has only ephemeral keys (see Section 6.1.2).

6.1.1 Each Party Has a Static Key Pair and Generates an Ephemeral Key Pair, C(2, 2)

For these schemes, each party (U and V) has a static key pair and generates an ephemeral key pair during the key agreement process. All key pairs **shall** be generated using the same domain parameters. Party U and party V obtain each other's static public keys, which have been generated prior to the key establishment process. Both parties generate ephemeral private/public key pairs and exchange the ephemeral public keys. Using the static and ephemeral keys, both parties generate a shared secret. The shared secret keying material is derived from the shared secret (see Figure 4).

Prerequisites: The following are prerequisites for the use of all C(2, 2) schemes.

1. Each party **shall** have an authentic copy of the same set of domain parameters, D. These parameters **shall** have been generated as specified in Section 5.5.1. For FFC schemes, $D = (p, q, g\{, SEED, pgenCounter\})$; for ECC schemes, $D = (q, FR, a, b\{, SEED\}, G, n, h)$. Furthermore, each party **shall** have assurance of the validity of these domain parameters as specified in Section 5.5.2.

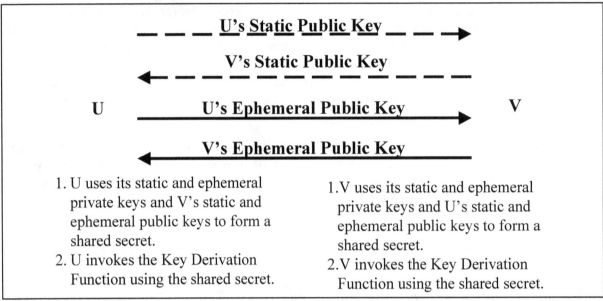

Figure 4: General Protocol when Each Party Generates Both Static and Ephemeral Key Pairs

2. Each party **shall** have been designated as the owner of a static key pair that was generated as specified in Section 5.6.1 using the set of domain parameters, D. For FFC schemes, the static key pair is (x, y); for ECC schemes, the static key pair is (d_s, Q_s). Each party **shall** obtain assurance of the validity of its own static public key as specified in Section 5.6.2.1. Each party **shall** obtain assurance of its possession of the correct value for its own private key as specified in Section 5.6.3.1.

3. The parties **shall** have agreed upon an Approved key derivation function (see Section 5.8) as well as an Approved hash function appropriate for use with the key derivation function and associated parameters (see Section 5.5). If key confirmation is used, the parties **shall** have agreed upon an Approved MAC and associated parameters (see Tables 1 and 2).

4. Prior to or during the key agreement process, each party **shall** obtain the identifier associated with the other party during the key agreement scheme and the static public key that is bound to that identifier. These static public keys **shall** be obtained in a trusted manner (e.g., from a certificate signed by a trusted CA). Each party **shall** obtain assurance of the validity of the other party's static public key as specified in Section 5.6.2.2

The recipient of a static public key **shall** obtain assurance that its (claimed) owner is (or was) in possession of the corresponding static private key, as specified in Section 5.6.3.2.

6.1.1.1 dhHybrid1, C(2, 2, FFC DH)

This section describes the dhHybrid1 scheme from ANS X9.42. The prerequisites for this scheme **shall** be satisfied as specified in Section 6.1.1. In particular, party U **shall** obtain the static public key y_V of party V, and party V **shall** obtain the static public key y_U of party U.

With the exception of key derivation, dhHybrid1 is "symmetric" in the actions of parties U (the initiator) and V (the responder). Only the actions performed by party U are specified here; a specification of the actions performed by party V may be obtained by systematically replacing the symbol "U" by "V" (and vice versa) in the description of the key agreement transformation. Note, however, that U and V must use identical orderings of the bit strings that are input to the key derivation function.

Party U **shall** execute the following key agreement transformation in order to a) establish a shared secret value Z with party V, and b) derive shared secret keying material from Z.

Actions: U **shall** derive secret keying material as follows:

1. Generate an ephemeral key pair (r_U, t_U) from the domain parameters D as specified in Section 5.6.1. Send the public key t_U to V. Receive an ephemeral public key t_V (purportedly) from V. If t_V is not received, output an error indicator and stop.

2. Verify that t_V is a valid public key for the parameters D as specified in Section 5.6.2.3. If assurance of public key validity cannot be obtained, output an error indicator and stop.

3. Use the FFC DH primitive in Section 5.7.1.1 to derive a shared secret Z_s – an integer in the range [2, p-2] – from the set of domain parameters D, U's static private key x_U, and V's static public key y_V. Convert Z_s to a byte string (which is also denoted by Z_s) using the Integer-to-Byte-String Conversion specified in Appendix C.1, and then zeroize the results of all intermediate calculations used in the computation of Z_s. If the call to the FFC DH primitive outputs an error indicator, zeroize the results of all intermediate calculations used in the attempted computation of Z_s, output an error indicator, and stop.

4. Use the FCC DH primitive to derive a shared secret Z_e – another integer in the range [2, p-2] – from the set of domain parameters D, U's ephemeral private key r_U, and V's ephemeral public key t_V. Convert Z_e to a byte string (which is also denoted by Z_e) using the Integer-to-Byte-String Conversion specified in Appendix C.1, and then zeroize the results of all intermediate calculations used in the computation of Z_e. If this call to the FFC DH primitive outputs an error indicator, zeroize Z_s and the results of all intermediate calculations used in the attempted computation of Z_e, output an error indicator, and stop.

5. Compute the shared secret $Z = Z_e \| Z_s$. Zeroize the results of all intermediate calculations used in the computation of Z (including Z_e and Z_s).

6. Use the agreed-upon key derivation function to derive secret keying material *DerivedKeyingMaterial* of length *keydatalen* bits from the shared secret value Z and *OtherInput* (including the identifiers ID_U and ID_V). (See Section 5.8.) If the key

derivation function outputs an error indicator, zeroize all copies of Z, output an error indicator, and stop.

7. Zeroize all copies of the shared secret Z and output *DerivedKeyingMaterial*.

Output: The bit string *DerivedKeyingMaterial* of length *keydatalen* bits or an error indicator.

Note: If key confirmation is to be incorporated into this scheme, additional input may be required, and additional steps must be taken by U and V beyond the computation of *DerivedKeyingMaterial*. See Section 8 for details.

dhHybrid1 is summarized in Table 6.

Table 6: dhHybrid1 Key Agreement Scheme Summary

	Party U	Party V
Domain Parameters	$D = (p, q, g\{, SEED, pgenCounter\})$	$D = (p, q, g\{, SEED, pgenCounter\})$
Static Data	1. Static private key x_U 2. Static public key y_U	1. Static private key x_V 2. Static public key y_V
Ephemeral Data	1. Ephemeral private key r_U 2. Ephemeral public key t_U	1. Ephemeral private key r_V 2. Ephemeral public key t_V
Computation	Compute Z_s by calling FFC DH using x_U and y_V Compute Z_e by calling FFC DH using r_U and t_V Compute $Z = Z_e \| Z_s$	Compute Z_s by calling FFC DH using x_V and y_U Compute Z_e by calling FFC DH using r_V and t_U Compute $Z = Z_e \| Z_s$
Derive Secret Keying Material	Compute kdf(Z,*OtherInput*) Zeroize Z	Compute kdf(Z,*OtherInput*) Zeroize Z

6.1.1.2 Full Unified Model, C(2, 2, ECC CDH)

This section describes the Full Unified Model scheme from ANS X9.63. The prerequisites for this scheme **shall** be satisfied as specified in Section 6.1.1. In particular, party U **shall** obtain the static public key $Q_{s,V}$ of party V, and party V **shall** obtain the static public key $Q_{s,U}$ of party U.

With the exception of key derivation, Full Unified Model is "symmetric" in the actions of parties U (the initiator) and V (the responder). Only the actions performed by party U are specified here;

a specification of the actions performed by party V may be obtained by systematically replacing the symbol "U" by "V" (and vice versa) in the description of the key agreement transformation. Note, however, that U and V must use identical orderings of the bit strings that are input to the key derivation function.

Party U **shall** execute the following key agreement transformation in order to a) establish a shared secret value Z with party V, and b) derive shared secret keying material from Z.

Actions: U **shall** derive secret keying material as follows:

1. Generate an ephemeral key pair $(d_{e,U}, Q_{e,U})$ from the domain parameters D as specified in Section 5.6.1. Send the public key $Q_{e,U}$ to V. Receive an ephemeral public key $Q_{e,V}$ (purportedly) from V. If $Q_{e,V}$ is not received, output an error indicator and stop.

2. Verify that $Q_{e,V}$ is a valid public key for the parameters D as specified in Section 5.6.2.3. If assurance of public key validity cannot be obtained, output an error indicator and stop.

3. Use the ECC CDH primitive in Section 5.7.1.2 to derive a shared secret Z_s – an element of the finite field of size q – from the set of domain parameters D, U's static private key $d_{s,U}$, and V's static public key $Q_{s,V}$. Convert Z_s to a byte string (which is also denoted by Z_s) using the Field-element-to-Byte-String Conversion specified in Appendix C.2, and then zeroize the results of all intermediate calculations used in the computation of Z_s. If the call to the ECC CDH primitive outputs an error indicator, zeroize the results of all intermediate calculations used in the attempted computation of Z_s, output an error indicator, and stop.

4. Use the ECC CDH primitive to derive a shared secret Z_e – another element of the finite field of size q – from the set of domain parameters D, U's ephemeral private key $d_{e,U}$ and V's ephemeral public key $Q_{e,V}$. Convert Z_e to a byte string (which is also denoted by Z_e) using the Field-element-to-Byte-String Conversion specified in Appendix C.2, and then zeroize the results of all intermediate calculations used in the computation of Z_e. If this call to the ECC CDH primitive outputs an error indicator, zeroize Z_s and the results of all intermediate calculations used in the attempted computation of Z_e, output an error indicator, and stop.

5. Compute the shared secret $Z = Z_e \| Z_s$. Zeroize the results of all intermediate calculations used in the computation of Z (including Z_e and Z_s).

6. Use the agreed-upon key derivation function to derive secret keying material *DerivedKeyingMaterial* of length *keydatalen* bits from the shared secret value Z and *OtherInput* (including the identifiers ID_U and ID_V). (See Section 5.8.) If the key derivation function outputs an error indicator, zeroize all copies of Z, output an error indicator, and stop.

7. Zeroize all copies of the shared secret Z and output *DerivedKeyingMaterial*.

Output: The bit string *DerivedKeyingMaterial* of length *keydatalen* bits or an error indicator.

Note: If key confirmation is to be incorporated into this scheme, additional input may be required, and additional steps must be taken by U and V beyond the computation of *DerivedKeyingMaterial*. See Section 8 for details.

The Full Unified Model is summarized in Table 7.

Table 7: Full Unified Model Key Agreement Scheme Summary

	Party U	**Party V**
Domain Parameters	$D = (q, FR, a, b\{, SEED\}, G, n, h)$	$D = (q, FR, a, b\{, SEED\}, G, n, h)$
Static Data	1. Static private key $d_{s,U}$ 2. Static public key $Q_{s,U}$	1. Static private key $d_{s,V}$ 2. Static public key $Q_{s,V}$
Ephemeral Data	1. Ephemeral private key $d_{e,U}$ 2. Ephemeral public key $Q_{e,U}$	1. Ephemeral private key $d_{e,V}$ 2. Ephemeral public key $Q_{e,V}$
Computation	Compute Z_s by calling ECC CDH using $d_{s,U}$ and $Q_{s,V}$ Compute Z_e by calling ECC CDH using $d_{e,U}$ and $Q_{e,V}$ Compute $Z = Z_e \| Z_s$	Compute Z_s by calling ECC CDH using $d_{s,V}$ and $Q_{s,U}$ Compute Z_e by calling ECC CDH using $d_{e,V}$ and $Q_{e,U}$ Compute $Z = Z_e \| Z_s$
Derive Secret Keying Material	Compute kdf(Z,*OtherInput*) Zeroize Z	Compute kdf(Z,*OtherInput*) Zeroize Z

6.1.1.3 MQV2, C(2, 2, FFC MQV)

This section describes the MQV2 scheme from ANS X9.42. The prerequisites for this scheme **shall** be satisfied as specified in Section 6.1.1. In particular, party U **shall** obtain the static public key y_V of party V, and party V **shall** obtain the static public key y_U of party U.

With the exception of key derivation, MQV2 is "symmetric" in the actions of parties U (the initiator) and V (the responder). Only the actions performed by party U are specified here; a specification of the actions performed by party V may be obtained by systematically replacing the symbol "U" by "V" (and vice versa) in the description of the key agreement transformation. Note, however, that U and V must use identical orderings of the bit strings that are input to the key derivation function.

Party U **shall** execute the following key agreement transformation in order to a) establish a shared secret value Z with party V, and b) derive shared secret keying material from Z.

Actions: U **shall** derive secret keying material as follows:

1. Generate an ephemeral key pair (r_U, t_U) from the domain parameters D as specified in Section 5.6.1.1. Send the public key t_U to V. Receive an ephemeral public key t_V (purportedly) from V. If t_V is not received, output an error indicator and stop.

2. Verify that t_V is a valid public key for the parameters D as specified in Section 5.6.2.3. If assurance of public key validity cannot be obtained, output an error indicator and stop.

3. Use the MQV2 form of the FFC MQV primitive in Section 5.7.2.1 to derive a shared secret Z – an integer in the range [2, p-2] – from the set of domain parameters D, U's static private key x_U, V's static public key y_V, U's ephemeral private key r_U, U's ephemeral public key t_U, and V's ephemeral public key t_V. If the call to the FFC MQV primitive outputs an error indicator, zeroize the results of all intermediate calculations used in the attempted computation of Z, output an error indicator, and stop.

4. Convert Z to a byte string (which is also denoted by Z) using the Integer-to-Byte-String Conversion specified in Appendix C.1, and then zeroize the results of all intermediate calculations used in the computation of Z.

5. Use the agreed-upon key derivation function to derive secret keying material *DerivedKeyingMaterial* of length *keydatalen* bits from the shared secret value Z and *OtherInput* (including the identifiers ID_U and ID_V). (See Section 5.8.) If the key derivation function outputs an error indicator, zeroize all copies of Z, output an error indicator, and stop.

6. Zeroize all copies of the shared secret Z and output *DerivedKeyingMaterial*.

Output: The bit string *DerivedKeyingMaterial* of length *keydatalen* bits or an error indicator.

Note: If key confirmation is to be incorporated into this scheme, additional input may be required, and additional steps must be taken by U and V beyond the computation of *DerivedKeyingMaterial*. See Section 8 for details.

MQV2 is summarized in Table 8.

Table 8: MQV2 Key Agreement Scheme Summary

	Party U	**Party V**
Domain Parameters	$D = (p, q, g\{, SEED, pgenCounter\})$	$D = (p, q, g\{, SEED, pgenCounter\})$
Static Data	1. Static private key x_U 2. Static public key y_U	1. Static private key x_V 2. Static public key y_V

Ephemeral Data	1. Ephemeral private key r_U 2. Ephemeral public key t_U	1. Ephemeral private key r_V 2. Ephemeral public key t_V
Computation	Compute Z by calling FFC MQV using x_U, y_V, r_U, t_U, and t_V	Compute Z by calling FFC MQV using x_V, y_U, r_V, t_V, and t_U
Derive Secret Keying Material	Compute kdf(Z, *OtherInput*) Zeroize Z	Compute kdf(Z, *OtherInput*) Zeroize Z

6.1.1.4 Full MQV, C(2, 2, ECC MQV)

This section describes the Full MQV scheme from ANS X9.63. The prerequisites for this scheme **shall** be satisfied as specified in Section 6.1.1. In particular, party U **shall** obtain the static public key $Q_{s,V}$ of party V, and party V **shall** obtain the static public key $Q_{s,U}$ of party U.

With the exception of key derivation, the Full MQV scheme is "symmetric" in the actions of parties U (the initiator) and V (the responder). Only the actions performed by party U are specified here; a specification of the actions performed by party V may be obtained by systematically replacing the symbol "U" by "V" (and vice versa) in the description of the key agreement transformation. Note, however, that U and V must use identical orderings of the bit strings that are input to the key derivation function.

Party *U* **shall** execute the following transformation to a) establish a shared secret value Z with party V, and b) derive shared secret keying material from Z.

Actions: U **shall** derive secret keying material as follows:

1. Generate an ephemeral key pair $(d_{e,U}, Q_{e,U})$ from the domain parameters D as specified in Section 5.6.1.2. Send the public key $Q_{e,U}$ to V. Receive an ephemeral public key $Q_{e,V}$ (purportedly) from V. If $Q_{e,V}$ is not received, output an error indicator and stop.

2. Verify that $Q_{e,V}$ is a valid public key for the parameters D as specified in Section 5.6.2.3. If assurance of public key validity cannot be obtained, output an error indicator and stop.

3. Use the Full MQV form of the ECC MQV primitive in Section 5.7.2.3.1 to derive a shared secret value Z – an element of the finite field of size q – from the set of domain parameters D, U's static private key $d_{s,U}$, V's static public key $Q_{s,V}$, U's ephemeral private key $d_{e,U}$, U's ephemeral public key $Q_{e,U}$, and V's ephemeral public key $Q_{e,V}$. If the call to the ECC MQV primitive outputs an error indicator, zeroize the results of all intermediate calculations used in the attempted computation of Z, output an error indicator, and stop.

4. Convert Z to a byte string (which is also denoted by Z) using the Field-element-to-Byte String Conversion specified in Appendix C.2, and then zeroize the results of all intermediate calculations used in the computation of Z.

5. Use the agreed-upon key derivation function to derive secret keying material *DerivedKeyingMaterial* of length *keydatalen* bits from the shared secret value Z and *OtherInput* (including the identifiers ID_U and ID_V). (See Section 5.8.) If the key derivation function outputs an error indicator, zeroize all copies of Z, output an error indicator, and stop.

6. Zeroize all copies of the shared secret Z and output *DerivedKeyingMaterial*.

Output: The bit string *DerivedKeyingMaterial* of length *keydatalen* bits or an error indicator.

Note: If key confirmation is to be incorporated into this scheme, additional input may be required, and additional steps must be taken by U and V beyond the computation of *DerivedKeyingMaterial*. See Section 8 for details.

The Full MQV is summarized in Table 9.

Table 9: Full MQV Key Agreement Scheme Summary

	Party U	Party V
Domain Parameters	$D = (q, FR, a, b\{, SEED\}, G, n, h)$	$D = (q, FR, a, b\{, SEED\}, G, n, h)$
Static Data	1. Static private key $d_{s,U}$ 2. Static public key $Q_{s,U}$	1. Static private key $d_{s,V}$ 2. Static public key $Q_{s,V}$
Ephemeral Data	1. Ephemeral private key $d_{e,U}$ 2. Ephemeral public key $Q_{e,U}$	1. Ephemeral private key $d_{e,V}$ 2. Ephemeral public key $Q_{e,V}$
Computation	Compute Z by calling ECC MQV using $d_{s,U}$, $Q_{s,V}$, $d_{e,U}$, $Q_{e,U}$, and $Q_{e,V}$	Compute Z by calling ECC MQV using $d_{s,V}$, $Q_{s,U}$, $d_{e,V}$, $Q_{e,V}$, and $Q_{e,U}$
Derive Secret Keying Material	Compute kdf(Z,*OtherInput*) Zeroize Z	Compute kdf(Z,*OtherInput*) Zeroize Z

6.1.1.5 Rationale for Choosing a C(2, 2) Scheme

Since these schemes use two static keys, each party has assurance that no unintended party can compute the shared secret without the compromise of a static private key.

Since these schemes use two ephemeral keys, each party has assurance that the shared secret varies from one key establishment transaction to the next. Even if both static and ephemeral private keys of one party from one transaction are compromised, the shared secrets from other legitimate C(2, 2) transactions (that is, between honest parties) are still protected by the use of different ephemeral private keys.

Key confirmation can be provided in either or both directions for these schemes using the methods as specified in Sections 8.4.1, 8.4.2, and 8.4.3. Upon completion of a Key Confirmation as in Section 8, the recipient of the confirmation has assurance of the identifier of the key confirmation provider (through the identifier bound to the static key), as well as confirmation of the active participation of the provider.

For a given set of FFC domain parameters, MQV2 is expected to have better performance than dhHybrid1.

For a given set of ECC domain parameters, Full MQV is expected to have better performance than the Full Unified Model.

The MQV schemes (MQV2 and Full MQV) provide assurance to each party that if a malicious party compromises their static private key, the malicious party cannot masquerade as a third party to the party whose key was compromised. In other words, if a malicious party, E, compromises party A's static private key, then E cannot masquerade as any other party to A. The dhHybrid1 and Full Unified Model do not provide this assurance to either party. (Of course, for any scheme, if a static private key is compromised by an adversary, then that adversary can masquerade as the owner of that static private key to any other entity.)

6.1.2 Each Party Generates an Ephemeral Key Pair; No Static Keys are Used, C(2, 0)

For this category, only Diffie-Hellman schemes are specified. Each party generates ephemeral key pairs with the same domain parameters. The two parties exchange ephemeral public keys and then compute the shared secret. The secret keying material is derived using the shared secret (see Figure 5).

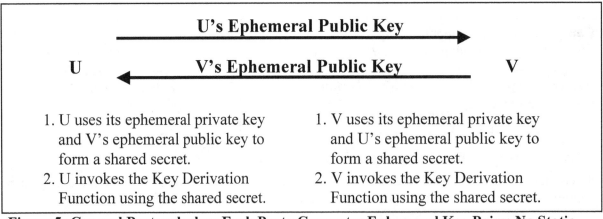

Figure 5: General Protocol when Each Party Generates Ephemeral Key Pairs; No Static Keys are Used

Prerequisites: The following are prerequisites for the use of all C(2, 0) schemes:

1. Each party **shall** have an authentic copy of the same set of domain parameters, D. These parameters **shall** have been generated as specified in Section 5.5.1. For FFC schemes, D = $(p, q, g\{, SEED, pgenCounter\})$; for ECC schemes, $D = (q, FR, a, b\{, SEED\}, G, n, h)$. Furthermore, each party **shall** have assurance of the validity of these domain parameters as specified in Section 5.5.2.

2. Each party **shall** have agreed upon an Approved key derivation function (see Section 5.8) as well as an Approved hash function appropriate for use with the key derivation function (see Section 5.5) with associated parameters.

3. Prior to or during the key agreement process, each party **shall** obtain the identifier associated with the other party during the key agreement scheme.

6.1.2.1 dhEphem, C(2, 0, FFC DH)

This section describes the dhEphem scheme from ANS X9.42. The prerequisites for this scheme **shall** be satisfied as specified in Section 6.1.2.

With the exception of key derivation, dhEphem is "symmetric" in the actions of parties U (the initiator) and V (the responder). Only the actions performed by party U are specified here; a specification of the actions performed by party V may be obtained by systematically replacing the symbol "U" by "V" (and vice versa) in the description of the key agreement transformation. Note, however, that U and V must use identical orderings of the bit strings that are input to the key derivation function.

Party U **shall** execute the following key agreement transformation in order to a) establish a shared secret value Z with party V, and b) derive shared secret keying material from Z.

Actions: U **shall** derive secret keying material as follows:

1. Generate an ephemeral key pair (r_U, t_U) from the domain parameters D as specified in Section 5.6.1. Send the public key t_U to V. Receive an ephemeral public key t_V (purportedly) from V. If t_V is not received, output an error indicator and stop.

2. Verify that t_V is a valid public key for the parameters D as specified in Section 5.6.2.3. If assurance of public key validity cannot be obtained, output an error indicator and stop.

3. Use the FCC DH primitive in Section 5.7.1.1 to derive a shared secret Z – an integer in the range [2, p-2] – from the set of domain parameters D, U's ephemeral private key r_U, and V's ephemeral public key t_V. If the call to the FFC DH primitive outputs an error indicator, zeroize the results of all intermediate calculations used in the attempted computation of Z, output an error indicator, and stop.

4. Convert Z to a byte string (which is also denoted by Z) using the Integer-to-Byte-String Conversion specified in Appendix C.1, and then zeroize the results of all intermediate calculations used in the computation of Z.

5. Use the agreed-upon key derivation function to derive secret keying material *DerivedKeyingMaterial* of length *keydatalen* bits from the shared secret value Z and

OtherInput (including the identifiers ID_U and ID_V). (See Section 5.8.) If the key derivation function outputs an error indicator, zeroize all copies of Z, output an error indicator, and stop.

6. Zeroize all copies of the shared secret Z and output *DerivedKeyingMaterial*.

Output: The bit string *DerivedKeyingMaterial* of length *keydatalen* bits or an error indicator.

dhEphem is summarized in Table 10.

Table 10: dhEphem Key Agreement Scheme Summary

	Party U	**Party V**
Domain Parameters	$(p, q, g\{, SEED, pgenCounter\})$	$(p, q, g\{, SEED, pgenCounter\})$
Static Data	N/A	N/A
Ephemeral Data	1. Ephemeral private key r_U 2. Ephemeral public key t_U	1. Ephemeral private key r_V 2. Ephemeral public key t_V
Computation	Compute Z by calling FFC DH using r_U and t_V	Compute Z by calling FFC DH using r_V and t_U
Derive Secret Keying Material	Compute kdf(Z,*OtherInput*) Zeroize Z	Compute kdf(Z,*OtherInput*) Zeroize Z

6.1.2.2 Ephemeral Unified Model, C(2, 0, ECC CDH)

This section describes the Ephemeral Unified Model scheme from ANS X9.63. The prerequisites for this scheme **shall** be satisfied as specified in Section 6.1.2.

With the exception of key derivation, Ephemeral Unified Model is "symmetric" in the actions of parties U (the initiator) and V (the responder). Only the actions performed by party U are specified here; a specification of the actions performed by party V may be obtained by systematically replacing the symbol "U" by "V" (and vice versa) in the description of the key agreement transformation. Note, however, that U and V must use identical orderings of the bit strings that are input to the key derivation function.

Party U **shall** execute the following key agreement transformation in order to a) establish a shared secret value Z with party V, and b) derive shared secret keying material from Z.

Actions: U **shall** derive secret keying material as follows:

1. Generate an ephemeral key pair $(d_{e,U}, Q_{e,U})$ from the domain parameters D as specified in Section 5.6.1. Send the public key $Q_{e,U}$ to V. Receive an ephemeral public key $Q_{e,V}$ (purportedly) from V. If $Q_{e,V}$ is not received, output an error indicator and stop.

2. Verify that $Q_{e,V}$ is a valid public key for the parameters D as specified in Section 5.6.2.3. If assurance of public key validity cannot be obtained, output an error indicator and stop.

3. Use the ECC CDH primitive in Section 5.7.1.2 to derive a shared secret Z – an element of the finite field of size q – from the set of domain parameters D, U's ephemeral private key $d_{e,U}$ and V's ephemeral public key $Q_{e,V}$. If the call to the ECC CDH primitive outputs an error indicator, zeroize the results of all intermediate calculations used in the attempted computation of Z, output an error indicator, and stop.

4. Convert Z to a byte string (which is also denoted by Z) using the Field-element-to-Byte-String Conversion specified in Appendix C.2, and then zeroize the results of all intermediate calculations used in the computation of Z.

5. Use the agreed-upon key derivation function to derive secret keying material *DerivedKeyingMaterial* of length *keydatalen* bits from the shared secret value Z and *OtherInput* (including the identifiers ID_U and ID_V). (See Section 5.8.) If the key derivation function outputs an error indicator, zeroize all copies of Z, output an error indicator, and stop.

6. Zeroize all copies of the shared secret Z and output *DerivedKeyingMaterial*.

Output: The bit string *DerivedKeyingMaterial* of length *keydatalen* bits or an error indicator..

The Ephemeral Unified Model is summarized in Table 11.

Table 11: Ephemeral Unified Model Key Agreement Scheme

	Party U	**Party V**
Domain Parameters	$(q, FR, a, b\{, SEED\}, G, n, h)$	$(q, FR, a, b\{, SEED\}, G, n, h)$
Static Data	N/A	N/A
Ephemeral Data	1. Ephemeral private key $d_{e,U}$ 2. Ephemeral public key $Q_{e,U}$	1. Ephemeral private key $d_{e,V}$ 2. Ephemeral public key $Q_{e,V}$
Computation	Compute Z by calling ECC CDH using $d_{e,U}$ and $Q_{e,V}$	Compute Z by calling ECC CDH using $d_{e,V}$ and $Q_{e,U}$
Derive Secret Keying Material	Compute kdf(Z, *OtherInput*) Zeroize Z	Compute kdf(Z, *OtherInput*) Zeroize Z

6.1.2.3 Rationale for Choosing a C(2, 0) Scheme

These schemes offer no assurance to either party of the identifier of the entity with whom they have established a shared secret, since there is no binding between an identifier and an ephemeral public key.

These schemes offer assurance to both parties that the current shared secret is isolated from prior and future compromises of shared secrets and private keys because all cryptographic material used in the computation of the shared secret is ephemeral and is zeroized immediately after use.

Despite the fact that these schemes offer very few assurances, they may be used as a component in a carefully constructed protocol. These schemes may be appropriate for applications where, for one reason or another, there is no need to know the identifier of the party with whom one is establishing a shared secret, or where the identifier is bound to the public key through some other method.

These schemes have the property of being relatively fast to compute, due to the lack of any certificate validation. They also require no support from a Certification Authority. These schemes are also often used as building blocks in larger protocols where other parts of the protocol add additional security properties.

This Recommendation does not specify how to add key confirmation to these schemes.

6.2 Schemes Using One Ephemeral Key Pair, C(1)

This category consists of two subcategories that are determined by the possession (or non-possession) of a static key pair by each of the parties. Let party U serve as the initiator, and party V serve as the responder. Only the initiator (party U) generates an ephemeral key pair. In the first subcategory, both the initiator and the responder have a static key pair, and the initiator also generates an ephemeral key pair (see Section 6.2.1). In the second subcategory, the initiator generates an ephemeral key pair, but has no static key pair; the responder has only a static key pair (see Section 6.2.2).

6.2.1 Initiator Has a Static Key Pair and Generates an Ephemeral Key Pair; Responder Has a Static Key Pair, C(1, 2)

For these schemes, party U (the initiator) uses both static and ephemeral private/public key pairs. Party V (the responder) uses only a static private/public key pair. Party U and party V obtain each other's static public keys in a trusted manner. Party U also sends its ephemeral public key to party V. A shared secret is generated by both parties using the available static and ephemeral keys. The shared secret keying material is derived using the shared secret (see Figure 6).

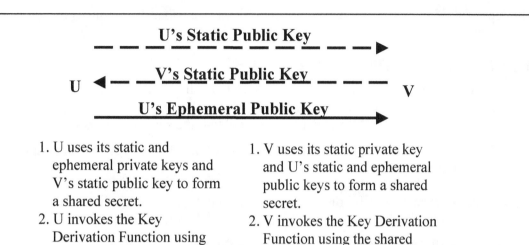

Figure 6: General Protocol when the Initiator has both Static and Ephemeral Key Pairs, and the Responder has only a Static Key Pair

Prerequisites: The following are prerequisites for the use of all C(1, 2) schemes.

1. Each party **shall** have an authentic copy of the same set of domain parameters, D. These parameters **shall** have been generated as specified in Section 5.5.1. For FFC schemes, $D = (p, q, g\{, SEED, pgenCounter\})$; for ECC schemes, $D = (q, FR, a, b\{, SEED\}, G, n, h)$. Furthermore, each party **shall** have assurance of the validity of these domain parameters as specified in Section 5.5.2.

2. Each party **shall** have been designated as the owner of a static key pair that was generated as specified in Section 5.6.1 using the set of domain parameters, D. For FFC schemes, the static key pair is (x, y); for ECC schemes, the static key pair is (d_s, Q_s). Each party **shall** obtain assurance of the validity of its own static public key as specified in Section 5.6.2.1. Each party **shall** obtain assurance of its possession of the correct value for its own private key as specified in Section 5.6.3.1.

3. The parties **shall** have agreed upon an Approved key derivation function (see Section 5.8) as well as an Approved hash function appropriate for use with the key derivation function and associated parameters (see Section 5.5). If key confirmation is used, the parties **shall** have agreed upon an Approved MAC and associated parameters (see Tables 1 and 2).

4. Prior to or during the key agreement process, each party **shall** obtain the identifier associated with the other party during the key agreement scheme and the static public key that is bound to that identifier. These static public keys **shall** be obtained in a trusted manner (e.g., from a certificate signed by a trusted CA). Each party **shall** obtain assurance of the validity of the other party's static public key as specified in Section 5.6.2.2.

The recipient of a static public key **shall** obtain assurance that its (claimed) owner is (or was) in possession of the corresponding static private key, as specified in Section 5.6.3.2.

6.2.1.1 dhHybridOneFlow, C(1, 2, FFC DH)

This section describes the dhHybridOneFlow scheme from ANS X9.42. The prerequisites for this scheme **shall** be satisfied as specified in Section 6.2.1. In particular, party U **shall** obtain the static public key y_V of party V, and party V **shall** obtain the static public key y_U of party U.

Note that U and V must use identical orderings of the bit strings that are input to the key derivation function.

Party U **shall** execute the following key agreement transformation in order to a) establish a shared secret value Z with party V, and b) derive shared secret keying material from Z.

Actions: U **shall** derive secret keying material as follows:

1. Generate an ephemeral key pair (r_U, t_U) from the domain parameters D as specified in Section 5.6.1. Send the public key t_U to V.

2. Use the FFC DH primitive in Section 5.7.1.1 to derive a shared secret Z_s – an integer in the range $[2, p\text{-}2]$ – from the set of domain parameters D, U's static private key x_U, and V's static public key y_V. Convert Z_s to a byte string (which is also denoted by Z_s) using the Integer-to-Byte-String Conversion specified in Appendix C.1, and then zeroize the results of all intermediate calculations used in the computation of Z_s. If the call to the FFC DH primitive outputs an error indicator, zeroize the results of all intermediate calculations used in the attempted computation of Z_s, output an error indicator, and stop.

3. Use the FCC DH primitive to derive a shared secret Z_e – another integer in the range $[2, p\text{-}2]$ – from the set of domain parameters D, U's ephemeral private key r_U, and V's static public key y_V. Convert Z_e to a byte string (which is also denoted by Z_e) using the Integer-to-Byte-String Conversion specified in Appendix C.1, and then zeroize the results of all intermediate calculations used in the computation of Z_e. If this call to the FFC DH primitive outputs an error indicator, zeroize Z_s and the results of all intermediate calculations used in the attempted computation of Z_e, output an error indicator, and stop.

4. Compute the shared secret $Z = Z_e \parallel Z_s$. Zeroize the results of all intermediate calculations used in the computation of Z (including Z_e and Z_s).

5. Use the agreed-upon key derivation function to derive secret keying material *DerivedKeyingMaterial* of length *keydatalen* bits from the shared secret value Z and *OtherInput* (including the identifiers ID_U and ID_V). (See Section 5.8.) If the key derivation function outputs an error indicator, zeroize all copies of Z, output an error indicator, and stop.

6. Zeroize all copies of the shared secret Z and output *DerivedKeyingMaterial*.

Output: The bit string *DerivedKeyingMaterial* of length *keydatalen* bits or an error indicator.

Party V **shall** execute the following key agreement transformation in order to a) establish a shared secret value Z with party U, and b) derive shared secret keying material from Z.

Actions: V **shall** derive secret keying material as follows:

1. Receive an ephemeral public key t_U (purportedly) from U. If t_U is not received, output an error indicator and stop.

2. Verify that t_U is a valid public key for the parameters D as specified in Section 5.6.2.3. If assurance of public key validity cannot be obtained, output an error indicator and stop.

3. Use the FFC DH primitive in Section 5.7.1.1 to derive a shared secret Z_s – an integer in the range $[2, p-2]$ – from the set of domain parameters D, V's static private key x_V, and U's static public key y_U. Convert Z_s to a byte string (which is also denoted by Z_s) using the Integer-to-Byte-String Conversion specified in Appendix C.1, and then zeroize the results of all intermediate calculations used in the computation of Z_s. If the call to the FFC DH primitive outputs an error indicator, zeroize the results of all intermediate calculations used in the attempted computation of Z_s, output an error indicator, and stop.

4. Use the FCC DH primitive to derive a shared secret Z_e – another integer in the range $[2, p-2]$ – from the set of domain parameters D, V's static private key x_V, and U's ephemeral public key t_U. Convert Z_e to a byte string (which is also denoted by Z_e) using the Integer-to-Byte-String Conversion specified in Appendix C.1, and then zeroize the results of all intermediate calculations used in the computation of Z_e. If this call to the FFC DH primitive outputs an error indicator, zeroize Z_s and the results of all intermediate calculations used in the attempted computation of Z_e, output an error indicator, and stop.

5. Compute the shared secret $Z = Z_e \| Z_s$. Zeroize the results of all intermediate calculations used in the computation of Z (including Z_e and Z_s).

6. Use the agreed-upon key derivation function to derive secret keying material *DerivedKeyingMaterial* of length *keydatalen* bits from the shared secret value Z and *OtherInput* (including the identifiers ID_U and ID_V). (See Section 5.8.) If the key derivation function outputs an error indicator, zeroize all copies of Z, output an error indicator, and stop.

7. Zeroize all copies of the shared secret Z and output *DerivedKeyingMaterial*.

Output: The bit string *DerivedKeyingMaterial* of length *keydatalen* bits or an error indicator.

Note: If key confirmation is to be incorporated into this scheme, additional input may be required, and additional steps must be taken by U and V beyond the computation of *DerivedKeyingMaterial*. See Section 8 for details.

dhHybridOneFlow is summarized in Table 12.

Table 12: dhHybridOneFlow Key Agreement Scheme Summary

	Party U	Party V
Domain Parameters	$(p, q, g\{, SEED, pgenCounter\})$	$(p, q, g\{, SEED, pgenCounter\})$
Static Data	1. Static private key x_U 2. Static public key y_U	1. Static private key x_V 2. Static public key y_V
Ephemeral Data	1. Ephemeral private key r_U 2. Ephemeral public key t_U	N/A
Computation	Compute Z_s by calling FFC DH using x_U and y_V Compute Z_e by calling FFC DH using r_U and y_V Compute $Z = Z_e \| Z_s$	Compute Z_s by calling FFC DH using x_V and y_U Compute Z_e by calling FFC DH using x_V and t_U Compute $Z = Z_e \| Z_s$
Derive Secret Keying Material	Compute kdf(Z, *OtherInput*) Zeroize Z	Compute kdf(Z, *OtherInput*) Zeroize Z

6.2.1.2 One-Pass Unified Model, C(1, 2, ECC CDH)

This section describes the One-Pass Unified Model scheme from ANS X9.63. The prerequisites for this scheme **shall** be satisfied as specified in Section 6.2.1. In particular, party U **shall** obtain the static public key $Q_{s,V}$ of party V, and party V **shall** obtain the static public key $Q_{s,U}$ of party U.

Note that U and V must use identical orderings of the bit strings that are input to the key derivation function.

Party U **shall** execute the following key agreement transformation in order to a) establish a shared secret value Z with party V, and b) derive shared secret keying material from Z.

Actions: U **shall** derive secret keying material as follows:

1. Generate an ephemeral key pair $(d_{e,U}, Q_{e,U})$ from the domain parameters D as specified in Section 5.6.1. Send the public key $Q_{e,U}$ to V.

2. Use the ECC CDH primitive in Section 5.7.1.2 to derive a shared secret Z_s – an element of the finite field of size q – from the set of domain parameters D, U's static private key

$d_{s,U}$, and V's static public key $Q_{s,V}$. Convert Z_s to a byte string (which is also denoted by Z_s) using the Field-element-to-Byte-String Conversion specified in Appendix C.2, and then zeroize the results of all intermediate calculations used in the computation of Z_s. If the call to the ECC CDH primitive outputs an error indicator, zeroize the results of all intermediate calculations used in the attempted computation of Z_s, output an error indicator, and stop.

3. Use the ECC CDH primitive to derive a shared secret Z_e – another element of the finite field of size q – from the set of domain parameters D, U's ephemeral private key $d_{e,U}$, and V's static public key $Q_{s,V}$. Convert Z_e to a byte string (which is also denoted by Z_e) using the Field-element-to-Byte-String Conversion specified in Appendix C.2, and then zeroize the results of all intermediate calculations used in the computation of Z_e. If this call to the ECC CDH primitive outputs an error indicator, zeroize Z_s and the results of all intermediate calculations used in the attempted computation of Z_e, output an error indicator, and stop.

4. Compute the shared secret $Z = Z_e \| Z_s$. Zeroize the results of all intermediate calculations used in the computation of Z (including Z_e and Z_s).

5. Use the agreed-upon key derivation function to derive secret keying material *DerivedKeyingMaterial* of length *keydatalen* bits from the shared secret value Z and *OtherInput* (including the identifiers ID_U and ID_V). (See Section 5.8.) If the key derivation function outputs an error indicator, zeroize all copies of Z, output an error indicator, and stop.

6. Zeroize all copies of the shared secret Z and output *DerivedKeyingMaterial*.

Output: The bit string *DerivedKeyingMaterial* of length *keydatalen* bits or an error indicator.

Party V **shall** execute the following key agreement transformation in order to a) establish a shared secret value Z with party U, and b) derive shared secret keying material from Z.

Actions: V **shall** derive secret keying material as follows:

1. Receive an ephemeral public key $Q_{e,U}$ (purportedly) from U. If $Q_{e,U}$ is not received, output an error indicator and stop.

2. Verify that $Q_{e,U}$ is a valid public key for the parameters D as specified in Section 5.6.2.3. If assurance of public key validity cannot be obtained, output an error indicator and stop.

3. Use the ECC CDH primitive in Section 5.7.1.2 to derive a shared secret Z_s – an element of the finite field of size q – from the set of domain parameters D, V's static private key $d_{s,V}$, and U's static public key $Q_{s,U}$. Convert Z_s to a byte string (which is also denoted by Z_s) using the Field-element-to-Byte-String Conversion specified in Appendix C.2, and then zeroize the results of all intermediate calculations used in the computation of Z_s. If the call to the ECC CDH primitive outputs an error indicator, zeroize the results of all intermediate calculations used in the attempted computation of Z_s, output an error indicator, and stop.

4. Use the ECC CDH primitive to derive a shared secret Z_e – another element of the finite field of size q – from the set of domain parameters D, V's static private key $d_{s,V}$, and U's ephemeral public key $Q_{e,U}$. Convert Z_e to a byte string (which is also denoted by Z_e) using the Field-element-to-Byte-String Conversion specified in Appendix C.2, and then zeroize the results of all intermediate calculations used in the computation of Z_e. If this call to the ECC CDH primitive outputs an error indicator, zeroize Z_s and the results of all intermediate calculations used in the attempted computation of Z_e, output an error indicator, and stop.

5. Compute the shared secret $Z = Z_e \parallel Z_s$. Zeroize the results of all intermediate calculations used in the computation of Z (including Z_e and Z_s).

6. Use the agreed-upon key derivation function to derive secret keying material *DerivedKeyingMaterial* of length *keydatalen* bits from the shared secret value Z and *OtherInput* (including the identifiers ID_U and ID_V). (See Section 5.8.) If the key derivation function outputs an error indicator, zeroize all copies of Z, output an error indicator, and stop.

7. Zeroize all copies of the shared secret Z and output *DerivedKeyingMaterial*.

Output: The bit string *DerivedKeyingMaterial* of length *keydatalen* bits or an error indicator.

Note: If key confirmation is to be incorporated into this scheme, additional input may be required, and additional steps must be taken by U and V beyond the computation of *DerivedKeyingMaterial*. See Section 8 for details.

The One-Pass Unified Model is summarized in Table 13.

Table 13: One-Pass Unified Model Key Agreement Scheme Summary

	Party U	Party V
Domain Parameters	$(q, FR, a, b\{, SEED\}, G, n, h)$	$(q, FR, a, b\{, SEED\}, G, n, h)$
Static Data	1. Static private key $d_{s,U}$ 2. Static public key $Q_{s,U}$	1. Static private key $d_{s,V}$ 2. Static public key $Q_{s,V}$
Ephemeral Data	1. Ephemeral private key $d_{e,U}$ 2. Ephemeral public key $Q_{e,U}$	N/A

	Party U	**Party V**
Computation	Compute Z_s by calling ECC CDH using $d_{s,U}$ and $Q_{s,v}$	Compute Z_s by calling ECC DH using $d_{s,v}$ and $Q_{s,U}$
	Compute Z_e by calling ECC CDH using $d_{e,U}$ and $Q_{s,v}$	Compute Z_e by calling ECC DH using $d_{s,v}$ and $Q_{e,U}$
	Compute $Z = Z_e \| Z_s$	Compute $Z = Z_e \| Z_s$
Derive Secret Keying Material	Compute kdf(Z,*OtherInput*)	Compute kdf(Z,*OtherInput*)
	Zeroize Z	Zeroize Z

6.2.1.3 MQV1, C(1, 2, FFC MQV)

This section describes the MQV1 scheme from ANS X9.42. The prerequisites for this scheme **shall** be satisfied as specified in Section 6.2.1. In particular, party U **shall** obtain the static public key y_V of party V, and party V **shall** obtain the static public key y_U of party U.

Note that U and V must use identical orderings of the bit strings that are input to the key derivation function.

Party U **shall** execute the following key agreement transformation in order to a) establish a shared secret value Z with party V, and b) derive shared secret keying material from Z.

Actions: U **shall** derive secret keying material as follows:

1. Generate an ephemeral key pair (r_U, t_U) from the domain parameters D as specified in Section 5.6.1. Send the public key t_U to V.

2. Use the MQV1 form of the FFC MQV primitive in Section 5.7.2.1 to derive a shared secret Z – an integer in the range [2, p-2] – from the set of domain parameters D, U's static private key x_U, V's static public key y_V, U's ephemeral private key r_U, U's ephemeral public key t_U, and (for a second time) V's static public key y_V. If the call to the FFC MQV primitive outputs an error indicator, zeroize the results of all intermediate calculations used in the attempted computation of Z, output an error indicator, and stop.

3. Convert Z to a byte string (which is also denoted by Z) using the Integer-to-Byte-String Conversion specified in Appendix C.1, and then zeroize the results of all intermediate calculations used in the computation of Z.

4. Use the agreed-upon key derivation function to derive secret keying material *DerivedKeyingMaterial* of length *keydatalen* bits from the shared secret value Z and *OtherInput* (including the identifiers ID_U and ID_V). (See Section 5.8.) If the key derivation function outputs an error indicator, zeroize all copies of Z, output an error indicator, and stop.

5. Zeroize all copies of the shared secret Z and output *DerivedKeyingMaterial*.

Output: The bit string *DerivedKeyingMaterial* of length *keydatalen* bits or an error indicator.

Party V **shall** execute the following key agreement transformation in order to a) establish a shared secret value Z with party U, and b) derive shared secret keying material from Z.

Actions: V **shall** derive secret keying material as follows:

1. Receive an ephemeral public key t_U (purportedly) from U. If t_U is not received, output an error indicator and stop.

2. Verify that t_U is a valid public key for the parameters D as specified in Section 5.6.2.3. If assurance of public key validity cannot be obtained, output an error indicator and stop.

3. Use the MQV1 form of the FFC MQV primitive in Section 5.7.2.1 to derive a shared secret Z – an integer in the range $[2, p\text{-}2]$ – from the set of domain parameters D, V's static private key x_V, U's static public key y_U, V's static private key x_V (for a second time), V's static public key y_V, and U's ephemeral public key t_U. If the call to the FFC MQV primitive outputs an error indicator, zeroize the results of all intermediate calculations used in the attempted computation of Z, output an error indicator, and stop.

4. Convert Z to a byte string (which is also denoted by Z) using the Integer-to-Byte-String Conversion specified in Appendix C.1, and then zeroize the results of all intermediate calculations used in the computation of Z.

5. Use the agreed-upon key derivation function to derive secret keying material *DerivedKeyingMaterial* of length *keydatalen* bits from the shared secret value Z and *OtherInput* (including the identifiers ID_U and ID_V). (See Section 5.8.) If the key derivation function outputs an error indicator, zeroize all copies of Z, output an error indicator, and stop.

6. Zeroize all copies of the shared secret Z and output *DerivedKeyingMaterial*.

Output: The bit string *DerivedKeyingMaterial* of length *keydatalen* bits or an error indicator.

Note: If key confirmation is to be incorporated into this scheme, additional input may be required, and additional steps must be taken by U and V beyond the computation of *DerivedKeyingMaterial*. See Section 8 for details.

MQV1 is summarized in Table 14.

Table 14: MQV1 Key Agreement Scheme Summary

	Party U	Party V
Domain Parameters	$(p, q, g\{, SEED, pgenCounter\})$	$(p, q, g\{, SEED, pgenCounter\})$
Static Data	1. Static private key x_U 2. Static public key y_U	1. Static private key x_V 2. Static public key y_V
Ephemeral Data	1. Ephemeral private key r_U 2. Ephemeral public key t_U	N/A
Computation	Compute Z by calling FFC MQV using x_U, y_V, r_U, t_U, and y_V (again)	Compute Z by calling FFC MQV using x_V, y_U, x_V (again), y_V, and t_U
Derive Secret Keying Material	Compute kdf(Z,*OtherInput*) Zeroize Z	Compute kdf(Z,*OtherInput*) Zeroize Z

6.2.1.4 One-Pass MQV, C(1, 2, ECC MQV)

This section describes the 1-Pass MQV scheme from ANS X9.63. The prerequisites for this scheme **shall** be satisfied as specified in Section 6.2.1. In particular, party U **shall** obtain the static public key $Q_{s,V}$ of party V, and party V **shall** obtain the static public key $Q_{s,U}$ of party U.

Note that U and V must use identical orderings of the bit strings that are input to the key derivation function.

Party U **shall** execute the following transformation to a) establish a shared secret value Z with party V, and b) derive shared secret keying material from Z.

Actions: U **shall** derive secret keying material as follows:

1. Generate an ephemeral key pair $(d_{e,U}, Q_{e,U})$ from the domain parameters D as specified in Section 5.6.1. Send the public key $Q_{e,U}$ to V.

2. Use the One-Pass MQV form of the ECC MQV primitive in Section 5.7.2.3.2 to derive a shared secret value Z – an element of the finite field of size q – from the set of domain parameters D, U's static private key $d_{s,U}$, V's static public key $Q_{s,V}$, U's ephemeral private key $d_{e,U}$, U's ephemeral public key $Q_{e,U}$, and (for a second time) V's static public key

$Q_{s,V}$. If the call to the ECC MQV primitive outputs an error indicator, zeroize the results of all intermediate calculations used in the attempted computation of Z, output an error indicator, and stop.

3. Convert Z to a byte string (which is also denoted by Z) using the Field-element-to-Byte String Conversion specified in Appendix C.2, and then zeroize the results of all intermediate calculations used in the computation of Z.

4. Use the agreed-upon key derivation function to derive secret keying material *DerivedKeyingMaterial* of length *keydatalen* bits from the shared secret value Z and *OtherInput* (including the identifiers ID_U and ID_V). (See Section 5.8.) If the key derivation function outputs an error indicator, zeroize all copies of Z, output an error indicator, and stop.

5. Zeroize all copies of the shared secret Z and output *DerivedKeyingMaterial*.

Output: The bit string *DerivedKeyingMaterial* of length *keydatalen* bits or an error indicator.

Party V **shall** execute the following transformation to a) establish a shared secret value Z with party U, and b) derive shared secret keying material from Z.

Actions: V **shall** derive secret keying material as follows:

1. Receive an ephemeral public key $Q_{e,U}$ (purportedly) from U. If $Q_{e,U}$ is not received, output an error indicator and stop.

2. Verify that $Q_{e,U}$ is a valid public key for the parameters D as specified in Section 5.6.2.3. If assurance of public key validity cannot be obtained, output an error indicator and stop.

3. Use the One-Pass MQV form of the ECC MQV primitive in Section 5.7.2.3 to derive a shared secret value Z – an element of the finite field of size q – from the set of domain parameters D, V's static private key $d_{s,V}$, U's static public key $Q_{s,U}$, V's static private key $d_{s,V}$ (for a second time), V's static public key $Q_{s,V}$, and U's ephemeral public key $Q_{e,U}$. If the call to the ECC MQV primitive outputs an error indicator, zeroize the results of all intermediate calculations used in the attempted computation of Z, output an error indicator, and stop.

4. Convert Z to a byte string (which is also denoted by Z) using the Field-element-to-Byte String Conversion specified in Appendix C.2, and then zeroize the results of all intermediate calculations used in the computation of Z.

5. Use the agreed-upon key derivation function to derive secret keying material *DerivedKeyingMaterial* of length *keydatalen* bits from the shared secret value Z and *OtherInput* (including the identifiers ID_U and ID_V). (See Section 5.8.) If the key derivation function outputs an error indicator, zeroize all copies of Z, output an error indicator, and stop.

6. Zeroize all copies of the shared secret Z and output *DerivedKeyingMaterial*.

Output: The bit string *DerivedKeyingMaterial* of length *keydatalen* bits or an error indicator.

Note: If key confirmation is to be incorporated into this scheme, additional input may be required, and additional steps must be taken by U and V beyond the computation of *DerivedKeyingMaterial*. See Section 8 for details.

The Full One-Pass MQV is summarized in Table 15.

Table 15: One-Pass MQV Model Key Agreement Scheme Summary

	Party U	**Party V**
Domain Parameters	$(q, FR, a, b\{, SEED\}, G, n, h)$	$(q, FR, a, b\{, SEED\}, G, n, h)$
Static Data	1. Static private key $d_{s,U}$ 2. Static public key $Q_{s,U}$	1. Static private key $d_{s,V}$ 2. Static public key $Q_{s,V}$
Ephemeral Data	1. Ephemeral private key $d_{e,U}$ 2. Ephemeral public key $Q_{e,U}$	N/A
Computation	Compute Z by calling ECC MQV using $d_{s,U}$, $Q_{s,V}$, $d_{e,U}$, $Q_{e,U}$, and $Q_{s,V}$ (again)	Compute Z by calling ECC MQV using $d_{s,V}$, $Q_{s,U}$, $d_{s,V}$ (again), $Q_{s,V}$, and $Q_{e,U}$
Derive Secret Keying Material	Compute kdf(Z, *OtherInput*) Zeroize Z	Compute kdf(Z, *OtherInput*) Zeroize Z

6.2.1.5 Rationale for Choosing a C(1, 2) Scheme

These schemes offer different assurances to the different parties participating in the exchange. One party (the initiator) has both static and ephemeral keys. The other party (the responder) has only a static key.

Both parties are assured that only they and the other intended party can compute the shared secret. The initiator, by virtue of its ephemeral contribution, has assurance that previous derived secret keying material will not be reused.

A compromise of the static private key of the initiator does not, by itself, compromise prior or future shared secrets (and therefore, secret keying material) of legitimate C(1, 2) transactions, nor does the compromise of only the initiator's ephemeral private key. However, the compromise of the static private key of the responder leads to the compromise of all future shared secrets where this party acts as a responder using the same static key. Additionally, any previous shared secrets (and therefore, secret keying material) that are computed with this party acting as responder become compromised if a malicious party stored the initiator's ephemeral public key.

For a given set of FFC domain parameters, MQV1 is expected to have better performance than the dhHybridOneFlow. For a given set of ECC domain parameters, One-Pass MQV is expected to have better performance than the One-Pass Unified Model.

Key confirmation can be provided in either or both directions using the methods specified in Sections 8.4.4, 8.4.5, and 8.4.6. Upon completion of a Key Confirmation as specified in Section 8, the recipient of the confirmation has assurance of the identifier of the key confirmation provider (through the identifier bound to the static key), as well as confirmation of the active participation of the provider

6.2.2 Initiator Generates Only an Ephemeral Key Pair; Responder Has Only a Static Key Pair, C(1, 1)

For these schemes, Party U generates an ephemeral key pair, but has no static key pair; party V has only a static key pair. Party U obtains party V's static public key in a trusted manner (for example, from a certificate signed by a trusted CA) and sends its ephemeral public key to Party V. The parties compute a shared secret using their private keys and the other party's public key. Each party uses the shared secret to derive secret keying material (see Figure 7).

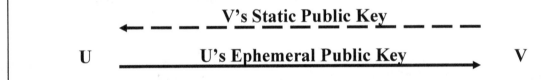

V's Static Public Key

U   **U's Ephemeral Public Key**   V

1. U uses its ephemeral private key and V's static public key to form a shared secret.
2. U invokes the Key Derivation Function using the shared secret.

1. V uses its static private key and U's ephemeral public key to form a shared secret.
2. V invokes the Key Derivation Function using the shared secret.

Figure 7: General Protocol when the Initiator has Only an Ephemeral Key Pair, and the Responder has Only a Static Key Pair

Prerequisites: The following are prerequisites for the use of all C(1, 1) schemes.

1. Each party **shall** have an authentic copy of the same set of domain parameters, D. These parameters **shall** have been generated as specified in Section 5.5.1. For FFC schemes, $D = (p, q, g\{, SEED, pgenCounter\})$; for ECC schemes, $D = (q, FR, a, b\{, SEED\}, G, n, h)$. Furthermore, each party **shall** have assurance of the validity of these domain parameters as specified in Section 5.5.2.

2. The responder **shall** have been designated as the owner of a static key pair that was generated as specified in Section 5.6.1 using the set of domain parameters, D. For FFC schemes, the static key pair is (x, y); for ECC schemes, the static key pair is (d_s, Q_s). The responder **shall** obtain assurance of the validity of its own static public key as specified in Section 5.6.2.1. The responder **shall** obtain assurance of its possession of the correct value of its own private key as specified in Section 5.6.3.1.

3. The parties **shall** have agreed upon an Approved key derivation function (see Section 5.8) as well as an Approved hash function appropriate for use with the key derivation function and associated parameters (see Section 5.5). If key confirmation is used, the parties **shall** have agreed upon an Approved MAC and associated parameters (see Tables 1 and 2).

4. Prior to or during the key agreement process, each party **shall** obtain the identifier associated with the other party during the key agreement scheme. The initiator **shall** obtain the static public key that is bound to the responder's identifier. This static public key **shall** be obtained in a trusted manner (e.g., from a certificate signed by a trusted CA). The initiator **shall** obtain assurance of the validity of the responder's static public key as specified in Section 5.6.2.2

The following is a prerequisite for using the derived keying material for purposes beyond the C(1,1) scheme itself.

The initiator **shall** obtain assurance that the responder is (or was) in possession of the appropriate static private key, as specified in Section 5.6.3.2.

6.2.2.1 dhOneFlow, C(1, 1, FFC DH)

This section describes the dhOneFlow scheme from ANS X9.42. The prerequisites for this scheme **shall** be satisfied as specified in Section 6.2.2. In particular, party U **shall** obtain the static public key y_V of party V.

Note that U and V must use identical orderings of the bit strings that are input to the key derivation function.

Party U **shall** execute the following key agreement transformation in order to a) establish a shared secret value Z with party V, and b) derive shared secret keying material from Z.

Actions: U **shall** derive secret keying material as follows:

1. Generate an ephemeral key pair (r_U, t_U) from the domain parameters D as specified in Section 5.6.1. Send the public key t_U to V.

2. Use the FCC DH primitive in Section 5.7.1.1 to derive a shared secret Z – an integer in the range $[2, p\text{-}2]$ – from the set of domain parameters D, U's ephemeral private key r_U, and V's static public key y_V. If the call to the FFC DH primitive outputs an error indicator, zeroize the results of all intermediate calculations used in the attempted computation of Z, output an error indicator, and stop.

3. Convert Z to a byte string (which is also denoted by Z) using the Integer-to-Byte-String Conversion specified in Appendix C.1, and then zeroize the results of all intermediate calculations used in the computation of Z.

4. Use the agreed-upon key derivation function to derive secret keying material *DerivedKeyingMaterial* of length *keydatalen* bits from the shared secret value Z and *OtherInput* (including the identifiers ID_U and ID_V). (See Section 5.8.) If the key derivation function outputs an error indicator, zeroize all copies of Z, output an error indicator, and stop.

5. Zeroize all copies of the shared secret Z and output *DerivedKeyingMaterial*.

Output: The bit string *DerivedKeyingMaterial* of length *keydatalen* bits or an error indicator.

Party V **shall** execute the following key agreement transformation in order to a) establish a shared secret value Z with party U, and b) derive shared secret keying material from Z.

Actions: V **shall** derive secret keying material as follows:

1. Receive an ephemeral public key t_U (purportedly) from U. If t_U is not received, output an error indicator and stop.

2. Verify that t_U is a valid public key for the parameters D as specified in Section 5.6.2.3. If assurance of public key validity cannot be obtained, output an error indicator and stop.

3. Use the FCC DH primitive in Section 5.7.1.1 to derive a shared secret Z – an integer in the range [2, p-2] – from the set of domain parameters D, V's static private key x_V and U's ephemeral public key t_U. If the call to the FFC DH primitive outputs an error indicator, zeroize the results of all intermediate calculations used in the attempted computation of Z, output an error indicator, and stop.

4. Convert Z to a byte string (which is also denoted by Z) using the Integer-to-Byte-String Conversion specified in Appendix C.1, and then zeroize the results of all intermediate calculations used in the computation of Z.

5. Use the agreed-upon key derivation function to derive secret keying material *DerivedKeyingMaterial* of length *keydatalen* bits from the shared secret value Z and *OtherInput* (including the identifiers ID_U and ID_V). (See Section 5.8.) If the key derivation function outputs an error indicator, zeroize all copies of Z, output an error indicator, and stop.

6. Zeroize all copies of the shared secret Z and output *DerivedKeyingMaterial*.

Output: The bit string *DerivedKeyingMaterial* of length *keydatalen* bits or an error indicator.

Note: If key confirmation is to be incorporated into this scheme, additional input may be required, and additional steps must be taken by U and V beyond the computation of *DerivedKeyingMaterial*. See Section 8 for details.

dhOneFlow is summarized in Table 16.

Table 16: dhOneFlow Key Agreement Scheme Summary

	Party U	Party V
Domain Parameters	$(p, q, g\{, SEED, pgenCounter\})$	$(p, q, g\{, SEED, pgenCounter\})$
Static Data	N/A	1. Static private key x_V 2. Static public key y_V
Ephemeral Data	1. Ephemeral private key r_U 2. Ephemeral public key t_U	N/A
Computation	Compute Z by calling FFC DH using r_U and y_V	Compute Z by calling FFC DH using x_V and t_U
Derive Secret Material	Compute kdf(Z,*OtherInput*) Zeroize Z	Compute kdf(Z,*OtherInput*) Zeroize Z

6.2.2.2 One-Pass Diffie-Hellman, C(1, 1, ECC CDH)

This section describes the One-Pass Diffie-Hellman scheme from ANS X9.63. The prerequisites for this scheme **shall** be satisfied as specified in Section 6.2.2. In particular, party U **shall** obtain the static public key $Q_{s,V}$ of party V.

Note that U and V must use identical orderings of the bit strings that are input to the key derivation function.

Party U **shall** execute the following key agreement transformation in order to a) establish a shared secret value Z with party V, and b) derive shared secret keying material from Z.

Actions: U **shall** derive secret keying material as follows:

1. Generate an ephemeral key pair $(d_{e,U}, Q_{e,U})$ from the domain parameters D as specified in Section 5.6.1. Send the public key $Q_{e,U}$ to V.

2. Use the ECC CDH primitive in Section 5.7.1.2 to derive a shared secret Z – an element of the finite field of size q – from the set of domain parameters D, U's ephemeral private key $d_{e,U,}$ and V's static public key $Q_{s,V}$. If this call to the ECC CDH primitive outputs an error indicator, zeroize the results of all intermediate calculations used in the attempted computation of Z, output an error indicator, and stop.

3. Convert Z to a byte string (which is also denoted by Z) using the Field-element-to-Byte-String Conversion specified in Appendix C.2, and then zeroize the results of all intermediate calculations used in the computation of Z.

4. Use the agreed-upon key derivation function to derive secret keying material *DerivedKeyingMaterial* of length *keydatalen* bits from the shared secret value Z and *OtherInput* (including the identifiers ID_U and ID_V). (See Section 5.8.) If the key derivation function outputs an error indicator, zeroize all copies of Z, output an error indicator, and stop.

5. Zeroize all copies of the shared secret Z and output *DerivedKeyingMaterial*.

Output: The bit string *DerivedKeyingMaterial* of length *keydatalen* bits or an error indicator.

Party V **shall** execute the following key agreement transformation in order to a) establish a shared secret value Z with party U, and b) derive shared secret keying material from Z.

Actions: V **shall** derive secret keying material as follows:

1. Receive an ephemeral public key $Q_{e,U}$ (purportedly) from U. If $Q_{e,U}$ is not received, output an error indicator and stop.

2. Verify that $Q_{e,U}$ is a valid public key for the parameters D as specified in Section 5.6.2.3. If assurance of public key validity cannot be obtained, output an error indicator and stop.

3. Use the ECC CDH primitive in Section 5.7.1.2 to derive a shared secret Z – an element of the finite field of size q – from the set of domain parameters D, V's static private key $d_{s,V,}$ and U's ephemeral public key $Q_{e,U.}$ If this call to the ECC CDH primitive outputs an error indicator, zeroize the results of all intermediate calculations used in the attempted computation of Z, output an error indicator, and stop.

4. Convert Z to a byte string (which is also denoted by Z) using the Field-element-to-Byte-String Conversion specified in Appendix C.2, and then zeroize the results of all intermediate calculations used in the computation of Z.

5. Use the agreed-upon key derivation function to derive secret keying material *DerivedKeyingMaterial* of length *keydatalen* bits from the shared secret value Z and *OtherInput* (including the identifiers ID_U and ID_V). (See Section 5.8.) If the key derivation function outputs an error indicator, zeroize all copies of Z, output an error indicator, and stop.

6. Zeroize all copies of the shared secret Z and output *DerivedKeyingMaterial*.

Output: The bit string *DerivedKeyingMaterial* of length *keydatalen* bits or an error indicator.

Note: If key confirmation is to be incorporated into this scheme, additional input may be required, and additional steps must be taken by U and V beyond the computation of *DerivedKeyingMaterial*. See Section 8 for details.

The One-Pass Diffie-Hellman is summarized in Table 17.

Table 17: One-Pass Diffie-Hellman Key Agreement Scheme Summary

	Party U	Party V
Domain Parameters	$(q, FR, a, b\{, SEED\}, G, n, h)$	$(q, FR, a, b\{, SEED\}, G, n, h)$
Static Data	N/A	1. Static private key $d_{s,V}$ 2. Static public key $Q_{s,V}$
Ephemeral Data	1. Ephemeral private key $d_{e,U}$ 2. Ephemeral public key $Q_{e,U}$	N/A
Computation	Compute Z by calling ECC CDH using $d_{e,U}$ and $Q_{s,V}$	Compute Z by calling ECC CDH using $d_{s,V}$ and $Q_{e,U}$
Derive Secret Keying Material	Compute kdf(Z, *OtherInput*) Zeroize Z	Compute kdf(Z, *OtherInput*) Zeroize Z

6.2.2.3 Rationale in Choosing a C(1, 1) Scheme

In these schemes, one party (the initiator) has only an ephemeral key, while the other party (the responder) has only a static key. Different assurances are given to the different parties in the key establishment transaction.

Due to the use of a static key by the responder, the initiator (only) has assurance that no unintended party can compute the shared secret without the compromise of private material. The responder has no such assurance, since the responder has no assurance about who is providing the ephemeral key (that is, unless there are additional appropriate elements in the protocol using this scheme).

Due to the use of an ephemeral key by the initiator, the initiator has assurance that a previous shared secret will not be reused.

There is no assurance to either party that the security of the shared secret is isolated from compromises of private keys from prior or future C(1, 1) transactions. A compromise of the initiator's ephemeral private key compromises the shared secret for that individual transaction only. However, a compromise of the responder's static private key compromises all shared secrets resulting from future C(1, 1) transactions in which that party is a responder, as well as any shared secrets resulting from prior C(1, 1) transactions for which a malicious party stored the ephemeral public keys.

The responder does not have any assurances as to the identifier of the initiator.

The responder may provide key confirmation to the initiator as specified in Section 8.4.7, giving the initiator assurance as to the identifier and active participation of the responder.

6.3   Scheme Using No Ephemeral Key Pairs, C(0, 2)

In this category, the parties use only static key pairs that have been generated using the same domain parameters. Each party obtains the other party's static public keys. A nonce **shall** be sent by party U (the initiator) to party V (the scheme responder) to ensure that the derived keying material is different for each key establishment transaction. The parties calculate the shared secret using their own static private key and the other party's static public key. Secret keying material is derived using the key derivation function, the shared secret, and the nonce (see Figure 8).

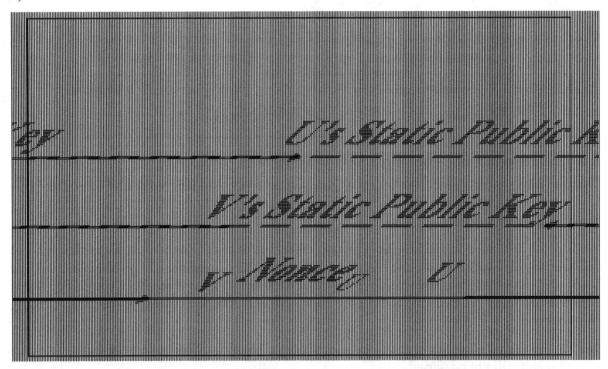

Figure 8: General Protocol when Each Party has only a Static Key Pair

Prerequisites: The following are prerequisites for the use of all C(0, 2) schemes.

1. Each party **shall** have an authentic copy of the same set of domain parameters, D. These parameters **shall** have been generated as specified in Section 5.5.1. For FFC schemes, $D = (p, q, g\{, SEED, pgenCounter\})$; for ECC schemes, $D = (q, FR, a, b\{, SEED\}, G, n, h)$. Furthermore, each party **shall** have assurance of the validity of these domain parameters as specified in Section 5.5.2.

2. Each party **shall** have been designated as the owner of a static key pair that was generated as specified in Section 5.6.1 using the set of Domain parameters, D. For FFC schemes,

the static key pair is (x, y); for ECC schemes, the static key pair is (d_s, Q_s). Each party **shall** obtain assurance of the validity of its own static public key as specified in Section 5.6.2.1. Each party **shall** obtain assurance of its possession of the correct value for its own private key as specified in Section 5.6.3.1.

3. The parties **shall** have agreed upon an Approved key derivation function (see Section 5.8) as well as an Approved hash function appropriate for use with the key derivation function and associated parameters (see Section 5.5). In addition the parties **shall** agree on the form of the nonce (see Section 5.4). If key confirmation is used, the parties **shall** have agreed upon the form of the an Approved MAC and associated parameters (see Tables 1 and 2).

4. Prior to or during the key agreement process, each party **shall** obtain the identifier associated with the other party during the key agreement scheme and the static public key that is bound to that identifier. These static public keys **shall** be obtained in a trusted manner (e.g., from a certificate signed by a trusted CA). Each party **shall** obtain assurance of the validity of the other party's static public key as specified in Section 5.6.2.2.

The recipient of a static public key **shall** obtain assurance that its (claimed) owner is (or was) in possession of the corresponding static private key, as specified in Section 5.6.3.2.

6.3.1 dhStatic, C(0, 2, FFC DH)

This section describes the dhStatic scheme from ANS X9.42. The prerequisites for this scheme **shall** be satisfied as specified in Section 6.3. In particular, party U **shall** obtain the static public key y_V of party V, and party V **shall** obtain the static public key y_U of party U.

Note that U and V must use identical orderings of the bit strings that are input to the key derivation function. In particular, this requirement applies to the placement of *Nonce$_U$* in the *PartyUInfo* subfield of *OtherInfo*.

Party U **shall** execute the following key agreement transformation in order to a) establish a shared secret value Z with party V, and b) derive shared secret keying material from Z.

Actions: U **shall** derive secret keying material as follows:

1. Obtain a nonce, *Nonce$_U$* (see Section 5.4). Send *Nonce$_U$* to V.

2. Use the FFC DH primitive in Section 5.7.1.1 to derive a shared secret Z – an integer in the range $[2, p\text{-}2]$ – from the set of domain parameters D, U's static private key x_U, and V's static public key y_V. If the call to the FFC DH primitive outputs an error indicator, zeroize the results of all intermediate calculations used in the attempted computation of Z, output an error indicator, and stop.

3. Convert Z to a byte string (which is also denoted by Z) using the Integer-to-Byte-String Conversion specified in Appendix C.1, and then zeroize the results of all intermediate calculations used in the computation of Z.

4. Use the agreed-upon key derivation function to derive secret keying material *DerivedKeyingMaterial* of length *keydatalen* bits from the shared secret value Z and *OtherInput* (including the identifiers IDu and IDv, and *Nonce$_U$*). *Nonce$_U$* **shall** be in the *PartyUInfo* subfield of *OtherInfo*. If the key derivation function outputs an error indicator, zeroize all copies of Z, output an error indicator, and stop.

5. Zeroize all copies of the shared secret Z and output *DerivedKeyingMaterial*.

Output: The bit string *DerivedKeyingMaterial* of length *keydatalen* bits or an error indicator.

Party V **shall** execute the following key agreement transformation in order to a) establish a shared secret value Z with party U, and b) derive shared secret keying material from Z.

Actions: V **shall** derive secret keying material as follows:

1. Obtain U's nonce, *Nonce$_U$,* from U. If *Nonce$_U$* is not available, output an error indicator and stop.

2. Use the FFC DH primitive in Section 5.7.1.1 to derive a shared secret Z – an integer in the range $[2, p\text{-}2]$ – from the set of domain parameters D, V's static private key $x_V,$ and U's static public key $y_U.$ If the call to the FFC DH primitive outputs an error indicator, zeroize the results of all intermediate calculations used in the attempted computation of Z, output an error indicator, and stop.

3. Convert Z to a byte string (which is also denoted by Z) using the Integer-to-Byte-String Conversion specified in Appendix C.1, and then zeroize the results of all intermediate calculations used in the computation of Z.

4. Use the agreed-upon key derivation function to derive secret keying material *DerivedKeyingMaterial* of length *keydatalen* bits from the shared secret value Z and *OtherInput* (including the identifiers ID_U and $ID_V,$ and *Nonce$_U$*). *Nonce$_U$* **shall** be in the *PartyUInfo* subfield of *OtherInfo*. If the key derivation function outputs an error indicator, zeroize all copies of Z, output an error indicator, and stop.

5. Zeroize all copies of the shared secret Z and output *DerivedKeyingMaterial*.

Output: The bit string *DerivedKeyingMaterial* of length *keydatalen* bits or an error indicator.

Note: If key confirmation is to be incorporated into this scheme, additional input may be required, and additional steps must be taken by U and V beyond the computation of *DerivedKeyingMaterial*. See Section 8 for details.

dhStatic is summarized in Table 18.

Table 18: dhStatic Key Agreement Scheme Summary

	Party U	Party V
Domain Parameters	$(p, q, g\{, SEED, pgenCounter\})$	$(p, q, g\{, SEED, pgenCounter\})$
Static Data	1. Static private key x_U 2. Static public key y_U	1. Static private key x_V 2. Static public key y_V
Ephemeral Data	$Nonce_U$	
Computation	Compute Z by calling FFC DH using x_U, and y_V	Compute Z by calling FFC DH using x_V, and y_U
Derive Secret Keying Material	Compute kdf(Z, *OtherInput*) using $Nonce_U$ Zeroize Z	Compute kdf(Z, *OtherInput*) using $Nonce_U$ Zeroize Z

6.3.2 Static Unified Model, C(0, 2, ECC CDH)

This section describes the Static Unified Model scheme from ANS X9.63. The prerequisites for this scheme **shall** be satisfied as specified in Section 6.3. In particular, party U **shall** obtain the static public key $Q_{s,V}$ of party V, and party V **shall** obtain the static public key $Q_{s,U}$ of party U.

Note that U and V must use identical orderings of the bit strings that are input to the key derivation function. The same requirement applies to the placement of $Nonce_U$ in the *PartyUInfo* subfield of *OtherInfo* (see item 4 below).

Party U **shall** execute the following key agreement transformation in order to a) establish a shared secret value Z with party V, and b) derive shared secret keying material from Z.

Actions: U **shall** derive secret keying material as follows:

1. Obtain a nonce, $Nonce_U$ (see Section 5.4). Send $Nonce_U$ to V.

2. Use the ECC CDH primitive in Section 5.7.1.2 to derive a shared secret Z – an element of the finite field of size q – from the set of domain parameters D, U's static private key $d_{s,U}$, and V's static public key $Q_{s,V}$. If the call to the ECC CDH primitive outputs an error indicator, zeroize the results of all intermediate calculations used in the attempted computation of Z, output an error indicator, and stop.

3. Convert Z to a byte string (which is also denoted by Z) using the Field-element-to-Byte-String Conversion specified in Appendix C.2, and then zeroize the results of all intermediate calculations used in the computation of Z.

4. Use the agreed-upon key derivation function to derive secret keying material *DerivedKeyingMaterial* of length *keydatalen* bits from the shared secret value Z and *OtherInput* (including the identifiers ID_U and ID_V, and $Nonce_U$). $Nonce_U$ **shall** be in the *PartyUInfo* sub field of *OtherInfo*. If the key derivation function outputs an error indicator, zeroize all copies of Z, output an error indicator, and stop.

5. Zeroize all copies of the shared secret Z and output *DerivedKeyingMaterial*.

Output: The bit string *DerivedKeyingMaterial* of length *keydatalen* bits or an error indicator.

Party V **shall** execute the following key agreement transformation in order to a) establish a shared secret value, Z, with party U, and b) derive shared secret keying material from Z.

1. Obtain U's nonce, $Nonce_U$, from U. If $Nonce_U$ is not if available, output an error indicator and stop.

2. Use the ECC CDH primitive in Section 5.7.1.2 to derive a shared secret Z – an element of the finite field of size q – from the set of domain parameters D, V's static private key $d_{s,V}$, and U's static public key $Q_{s,U}$. If the call to the ECC CDH primitive outputs an error indicator, zeroize the results of all intermediate calculations used in the attempted computation of Z, output an error indicator, and stop.

3. Convert Z to a byte string (which is also denoted by Z) using the Field-element-to-Byte-String Conversion specified in Appendix C.2, and then zeroize the results of all intermediate calculations used in the computation of Z_s.

4. Use the agreed-upon key derivation function to derive secret keying material *DerivedKeyingMaterial* of length *keydatalen* bits from the shared secret value Z and *OtherInput* (including the identifiers IDu and IDv, and $Nonce_U$). $Nonce_U$ **shall** be in the *PartyUInfo* subfield of *OtherInfo*. If the key derivation function outputs an error indicator, zeroize all copies of Z, output an error indicator, and stop.

5. Zeroize all copies of the shared secret Z and output *DerivedKeyingMaterial*.

Output: The bit string *DerivedKeyingMaterial* of length *keydatalen* bits or an error indicator.

Note: If key confirmation is to be incorporated into this scheme, additional input may be required, and additional steps must be taken by U and V beyond the computation of *DerivedKeyingMaterial*. See Section 8 for details.

Static Unified Model is summarized in Table 19.

Table 19: Static Unified Model Key Agreement Scheme Summary

	Party U	Party V
Domain Parameters	$(q, FR, a, b\{, SEED\}, G, n, h)$	$(q, FR, a, b\{, SEED\}, G, n, h)$
Static Data	1. Static private key $d_{s,U}$ 2. Static public key $Q_{s,U}$	1. Static private key $d_{s,V}$ 2. Static public key $Q_{s,V}$
Ephemeral Data	$Nonce_U$	
Computation	Compute Z by calling ECC CDH using $d_{s,U}$, and $Q_{s,V}$	Compute Z by calling ECC CDH using $d_{s,V}$, and $Q_{s,U}$
Derive Secret Keying Material	Compute kdf($Z, OtherInput$) using $Nonce_U$ Zeroize Z	Compute kdf($Z, OtherInput$) using $Nonce_U$ Zeroize Z

6.3.3 Rationale in Choosing a C(0, 2) Scheme

As identifiers are bound to the static public keys that are used, each party has assurance that the intended party and no other party can compute the shared secret, without the compromise of a private key. If an entity's private key is compromised, then all shared secrets of prior and future C(0, 2) transactions involving that party are compromised.

Both parties are assured that only they and the other intended party can compute the shared secret. The initiator, by virtue of $Nonce_U$, has assurance that previous derived secret keying material will not be reused.

Key confirmation can be provided in either or both directions for these schemes as specified in Sections 8.4.8, 8.4.9, and 8.4.10. Upon completion of a Key Confirmation, the recipient of the confirmation has assurance of the identifier of the key confirmation provider (through the identifier bound to the static key), as well as confirmation of the active participation of the provider.

7.   DLC-Based Key Transport

The FFC and ECC key agreement schemes in this Recommendation that employ a receiver's static key[6] may be followed by a key transport scheme using an Approved key-wrapping

---

[6] To prevent receiver identifier spoofing, since the sender would know the identifier of the intended receiver.

algorithm, such as the AES key-wrap algorithm [8]. In order to meet this requirement, DLC-based key transport **shall** be used with one of the following types of schemes:

1. C(2, 2) schemes,

2. C(1, 2) schemes,

3. C(1, 1), schemes with the receiver serving as the scheme responder, and

4. C(0, 2) schemes.

DLC-based key transport **shall not** be used with C(2, 0) schemes, or C(1, 1) schemes with the receiver serving as the scheme initiator.

The DLC-based key transport scheme is as follows:

1. A key agreement scheme is used to establish a shared secret and derive keying material between the sender and the receiver. Key confirmation (as specified in Section 8) may optionally be used to provide assurance that the shared secret is the same for both the initiator and responder.

2. The sender obtains a *KeyWrappingKey* from the *DerivedKeyingMaterial*.

3. The sender selects secret keying material, *KeyingMaterial*, to transport to the receiver.

4. The sender calculates *WrappedKey* = KeyWrap(*KeyWrappingKey, KeyingMaterial*) using KeyWrap( ), an Approved key wrapping algorithm.

5. The sender sends *WrappedKey* to the receiver.

6. The receiver receives *WrappedKey* from the sender.

7. The receiver obtains a *KeyWrappingKey* from the *DerivedKeyingMaterial* that is computed by applying the key derivation function to the shared secret.

8. The receiver calculates *KeyingMaterial* = KeyUnwrap(*KeyWrappingKey, WrappedKey*) using KeyUnwrap( ), the corresponding key unwrapping algorithm.

Note that if the key agreement scheme used in Step 1 is such that the receiver (acting as the responder) does not contribute an ephemeral key pair to the calculation of the shared secret (that is, either a C(1, 2), C(1, 1), or C(0, 2) scheme has been used), then Steps 1 through 5 can be performed by the sender (acting as the initiator) without direct involvement of the receiver. This can be useful in a store-and-forward environment, such as e-mail.

A default "rule" of this Recommendation is that ephemeral keys **shall not** be reused (see Section 5.6.4.3). An exception to this rule is that the sender may use the same ephemeral key pair in step 1 above in multiple DLC-based Key Transport transactions if the same secret keying material is being transported in each transaction and if all these transactions occur "simultaneously" (or within a short period of time). However, the security properties of the key establishment scheme may be affected by reusing the ephemeral key in this manner.

8. Key Confirmation

The term key confirmation refers to the use of explicit messages (such as messages containing the information defined in this Recommendation) to provide assurance to one party (the key confirmation *recipient*) that another party (the key confirmation *provider*) actually possesses the correct shared secret and/or derived keying material (from the key confirmation recipient's perspective). Key agreement, accompanied by key confirmation (as described in this Recommendation), can also be used to provide the recipient with assurance of either the provider's current or prior possession of the static private key that is associated with a particular static public key (see Section 8.1). A key establishment scheme is said to provide "**unilateral key confirmation**" when it provides this assurance to only one of the participants, and the scheme is said to provide "**bilateral key confirmation**" when this assurance is provided to both participants (that is, unilateral key confirmation is provided in both directions).

Oftentimes, key confirmation is provided implicitly by a means outside of the key establishment scheme (for example, by decrypting an encrypted message from the other party using a key derived from the shared secret), but this is not always the case. In some cases, it may be appropriate to include the exchange of explicit key confirmation information within the key establishment process itself. Key confirmation may enhance the security properties that are achieved by a key establishment scheme. For key confirmation to comply with this Recommendation, key confirmation **shall** be incorporated into key establishment schemes as specified in this section.

Unilateral key confirmation may be incorporated into any scheme that uses a static key pair associated with the provider. Successful key confirmation will provide assurance to the recipient that the provider has correctly derived keying material. Bilateral key confirmation may be added to any key agreement scheme in which each party possesses a static key pair.

Table 20 provides a summary of the scheme classes for which unilateral or bilateral key confirmation is specified. Note that key confirmation for the C(2, 0) key agreement schemes is not specified, since neither party has a static key pair; if needed, key confirmation would have to be provided by some other means.

Table 20: Key Agreement Schemes Using Unilateral and Bilateral Key Confirmation

Scheme Class	Unilateral	Bilateral
C(2, 2)	U to V, or V to U	Yes
C(2, 0)	No	No

Scheme Class	Unilateral	Bilateral
C(1, 2)	U to V, or V to U	Yes
C(1, 1)	V to U	No
C(0, 2)	U to V, or V to U	Yes

If key confirmation is incorporated into a scheme in which a recipient does not provide an ephemeral public key, a nonce **shall** be provided for the key confirmation process.

The process used to provide key confirmation requires string representations of the ephemeral public keys. The same notation will be used to represent these keys for schemes based on Finite Field cryptography (FFC) and elliptic curve cryptography (ECC):

$EphemPubKey_i$ = the byte string representation of a participant i's ephemeral public key.

For FFC schemes, an ephemeral public key, t_i, is converted from a field element in F_p to a byte string by representing the field element as an integer in the interval [2, p-2], and then converting the integer to a byte string as specified in Appendix C.1.

For ECC, the coordinates of the ephemeral public key, $Q_{e, i}$, are converted from field elements to byte strings as specified in Appendix C.2 and concatenated (with x first) to form a single byte string.

8.1   Assurance of Possession Considerations when using Key Confirmation

Key agreement, accompanied by key confirmation (as described in this Recommendation), can be used to provide the recipient with assurance of either the provider's current or prior possession of the static private key that is associated with a particular static public key. Current possession and prior possession are defined relative to the time of a particular key agreement transaction (including the delivery of the key confirmation message to the recipient).

As has been observed previously (see Section 5.6.3.2), an adequate demonstration of current possession of a static private key can be used to provide assurance that the claimed owner of a static key pair is the true owner. Note also that as time passes, even the true owner of a key pair may lose possession of the associated private key, either deliberately or due to an error. For these reasons, assurance of current possession can be of value for some applications. When it is desired (or required), assurance of current possession **shall** be obtained as specified below.

While assurance of prior possession may be sufficient for some purposes, if both assurance of current and prior possession are feasible to obtain, then assurance of current possession is preferred.

As stated in Section 5.6.3.2, in order for the recipient of a successful key confirmation to obtain assurance of the key confirmation provider's *current* possession of the static private key corresponding to the static public key claimed by that provider (and used in the key agreement transaction), the underlying key agreement scheme used **shall** be one of the following, and the recipient seeking assurance **shall** serve as the key agreement initiator:

- dhHybridOneFlow or (Cofactor) One-Pass Unified Model

- MQV1 or One-Pass MQV.

- dhOneFlow or (Cofactor) One-Pass Diffie-Hellman.

The key agreement scheme (including the key confirmation) **shall** be performed as described in this Recommendation.

In each of the schemes specified above, the key confirmation recipient contributes an ephemeral public key that is arithmetically combined with the static private key claimed by the provider as part of the provider's computation of the shared secret. The unpredictability of the ephemeral public key contributed by the recipient ensures that the provider's calculations are performed contemporaneously, and so a successful computation of the shared secret (as indicated through key confirmation) offers assurance that the provider has current possession of that static private key.

If the underlying key agreement scheme is not one of those indicated above (but is one of those described in this Recommendation), it is possible that some of the calculations required of the key confirmation provider (in particular, those portions depending on the provider's knowledge of a static private key) were completed at a time *prior* to the current key agreement transaction. (For example, if the key agreement scheme were either dhHybrid1or the Full Unified Model, the static shared secret Z_s could be computed in advance or recovered from a previous transaction.) The same is true if the key agreement scheme employed is one of those listed above, but the key confirmation recipient does not serve as the key agreement initiator. In such cases, the recipient of a successful key confirmation might obtain assurance that the key confirmation provider was — at some point in time — in possession of the static private key corresponding to the static public key claimed by that provider. However, the recipient would not obtain assurance that the provider actually had possession of the static private key during the current transaction.

8.2 Unilateral Key Confirmation for Key Agreement Schemes

Unilateral key confirmation occurs when one participant in a key establishment scheme (the "provider") provides assurance to the other participant (the "recipient") that the same shared secret has actually been generated by both the provider and the recipient, and thus provides assurance that shared keying material has been established between the provider and the recipient. This is an optional feature for any scheme in which the provider possesses a static key pair. If the intended key confirmation recipient does not contribute an ephemeral public key or nonce during the key establishment process, then a nonce **shall** be provided for key confirmation. Unilateral key confirmation may be added in either direction to the C(2, 2), C(1, 2) and C(0, 2) schemes; it may also be added to the C(1, 1) schemes, but in one direction only: when the scheme Responder (V) is the key confirmation provider, and the scheme Initiator (U) is the key confirmation recipient (see Table 20 in Section 8).

To include unilateral key confirmation from a provider (who has a static key pair) to a recipient, the following steps **shall** be incorporated into the scheme. Note that the provider may be either the scheme initiator (party U) or the scheme responder (party V), as long as the provider has a static key pair, and the recipient is the other party.

1. If the recipient does not have an ephemeral key pair and has not already provided a nonce as part of the scheme, then the recipient **shall** provide a nonce to be used in its place (see Section 5.4).

2. The provider computes

   $MacData_P = message\_string_P \parallel ID_P \parallel ID_R \parallel EphemData_P \parallel EphemData_R \{\parallel Text\}$

   where

   $message\_string_P$ is a six byte string with a value of "KC_1_U" or "KC_1_V" depending on whether U or V is providing the *MacTag*. Note that these values will differ for bilateral key confirmation in Section 8.3.

   ID_P is the identifier of the provider.

   ID_R is the identifier of the recipient.

   $EphemData_P =$ $EphemPubKey_P$ (if used in the key agreement scheme),

            $Nonce_P$ (if there is no $EphemPubKey_P$, and $Nonce_P$ is required to derive secret keying material, for example, when P is the initiator in a C(0, 2) scheme), or

            Null (otherwise), where *Null* is the empty byte string.

   $EphemData_R =$ $EphemPubKey_R$ (if used in the key agreement scheme)

            $Nonce_R$ (otherwise).

   $Text_1$ is an optional bit string that may be used during key confirmation and that is known by the parties establishing the secret keying material.

3. After computing the shared secret and applying the key derivation function to obtain *DerivedKeyingMaterial* (see Section 5.8), the provider parses *DerivedKeyingMaterial* into two parts, *MacKey* and *KeyData*:

   $MacKey \parallel KeyData = DerivedKeyingMaterial.$

4. The provider computes $MacTag_P$ (see Section 5.2.1) and sends it to the recipient:

   $MacTag_P = MAC (MacKey, MacLen, MacData_P).$

5. The recipient computes *MacData$_P$*, *MacKey*, *KeyData* and *MacTag$_P$* in the same manner as the provider, and then compares its computed *MacTag$_P$* to the value received from the provider. If the received value is equal to the derived value, then the recipient is assured that the provider has derived the same value for *MacKey* and that the provider shares the recipient's value of *MacTag$_P$*. The assurance of a shared value for *MacKey* provides assurance to the recipient that the provider also shares the secret value (*Z*) from which *MacKey* and *KeyData* are derived (see Section 5.8). Thus, the recipient also has assurance that the provider could compute *KeyData* correctly.

6. Zeroize the *MacKey*.

8.3   Bilateral Key Confirmation for Key Agreement Schemes

Bilateral key confirmation is obtained by performing unilateral key confirmation in both directions: from a provider U to a recipient V, and from a provider V to a recipient U. U and V may use different values for the optional *Text* in their *MacTag* computations, provided that both parties are aware of the value(s) used. *message_string$_P$* is a six byte string with a value of "KC_2_U" or "KC_2_V", depending on whether U or V is providing the *MacTag*. Bilateral key confirmation may be added to the C(2, 2), C(1, 2) and C(0, 2) schemes, as shown in the relevant subsections of Section 8.4.

8.4   Incorporating Key Confirmation into a Key Agreement Scheme

This section illustrates how to incorporate key confirmation (as described in Section 8.2 and Section 8.3 above) into specific key agreement schemes of Section 6.

The flow depictions separate the scheme flow from the key confirmation. The depictions and accompanying discussions assume that the prerequisites of the scheme have been satisfied, that the key agreement transaction has proceeded successfully (as described in Section 6) through the stage of key derivation, and that the received *MacTags* are successfully verified as specified in Section 5.2.2. If the *MacTags* do not verify, then key confirmation has not been obtained, and the key agreement transaction **shall** be discontinued.

8.4.1   C(2, 2) Scheme with Unilateral Key Confirmation Provided by U to V

Figure 9 depicts a typical flow for a C(2, 2) scheme with unilateral key confirmation from U to V. In this situation, party U, the scheme initiator, and party V, the scheme responder, assume the roles of key confirmation provider and recipient, respectively. The successful completion of this process provides party V with a) assurance that party U has derived the same secret *Z* value; and b) assurance that party U has actively participated in the process.

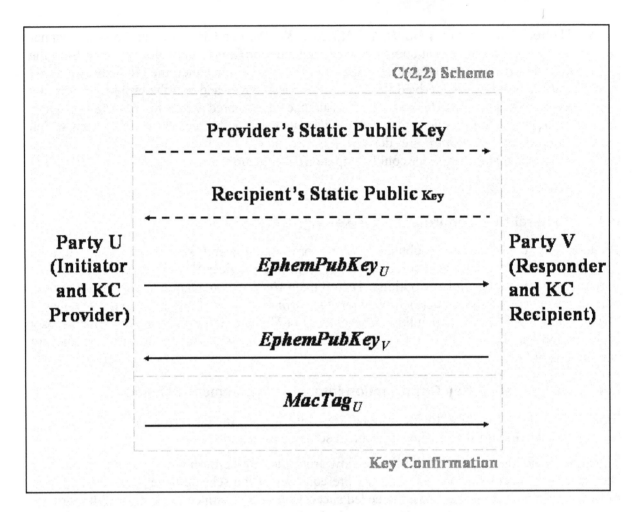

Figure 9: C(2, 2) Scheme with Unilateral Key Confirmation from Party U to Party V

To provide (and receive) key confirmation (as described in Section 8.2), U (and V) set $EphemData_U = EphemPubKey_U$, and $EphemData_V = EphemPubKey_V$:

Party U provides $MacTag_U$ to V (as specified in Section 8.2, with $P = U$ and $R = V$), where $MacTag_U$ is computed (as specified in Section 5.2.1) using

$MacData_U =$ "KC_1_U" $\| ID_U \| ID_V \| EphemPubKey_U \| EphemPubKey_V \{ \| Text \}$.

The recipient V uses the same format for $MacData_U$ to compute its own version of $MacTag_U$ and then verifies that the newly computed $MacTag_U$ matches the value provided by U.

8.4.2 C(2, 2) Scheme with Unilateral Key Confirmation Provided by V to U

Figure 10 depicts a typical flow for a C(2, 2) scheme with unilateral key confirmation from V to U. In this situation, party V, the scheme responder, and party U, the scheme initiator, assume the roles of key confirmation provider and recipient, respectively. The successful completion of the key confirmation process provides party U with a) assurance that party V has derived the same secret Z value; and b) assurance that party V has actively participated in the process.

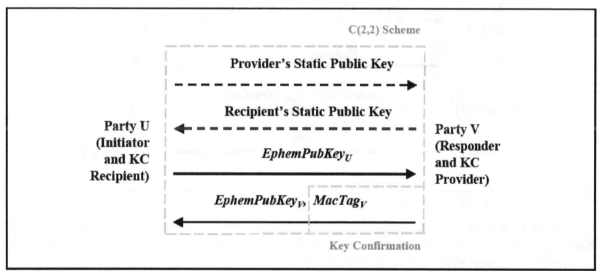

Figure 10: C(2, 2) Scheme with Unilateral Key Confirmation from Party V to Party U

To provide (and receive) key confirmation (as described in Section 8.2), V (and U) set $EphemData_V = EphemPubKey_V$, and $EphemData_U = EphemPubKey_U$:

Party V provides $MacTag_V$ to U (as specified in Section 8.2, with $P = V$ and $R = U$), where $MacTag_V$ is computed (as specified in Section 5.2.1) using

$MacData_V =$ "KC_1_V" $|| ID_V || ID_U || EphemPubKey_V || EphemPubKey_U \{|| Text\}$.

The recipient U uses the same format for $MacData_V$ to compute its own version of $MacTag_V$ and then verifies that the newly computed $MacTag_V$ matches the value provided by V.

Note that in Figure 10, party V's ephemeral public key ($EphemPubKey_V$) and the $MacTag$ ($MacTag_V$) are depicted as being sent in the same message (to reduce the number of passes in the combined key agreement/key confirmation process). They may also be sent separately.

8.4.3 C(2, 2) Scheme with Bilateral Key Confirmation

Figure 11 depicts a typical flow for a C(2, 2) scheme with bilateral key confirmation. In this method, party U, the scheme initiator, and party V, the scheme responder, assume the roles of both the provider and the recipient in order to obtain bilateral key confirmation. The successful completion of the key confirmation process provides each party with assurance that the other party has derived the same secret Z value, and also provides each party with assurance that the other party has actively participated in the process.

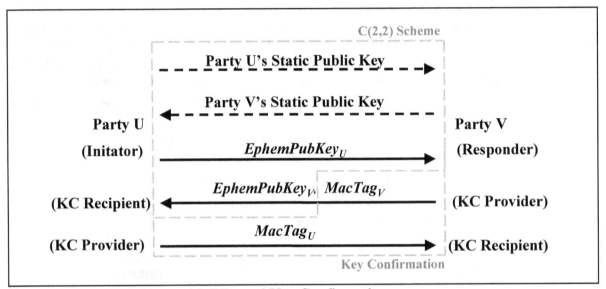

Figure 11: C(2, 2) Scheme with Bilateral Key Confirmation

To provide bilateral key confirmation (as described in Section 8.3), U and V exchange and verify *MacTags* that have been computed (as specified in Sections 5.2.1) using $EphemData_U = EphemPubKey_U$, and $EphemData_V = EphemPubKey_V$:

Party V provides $MacTag_V$ to U (as specified in Section 8.2, with $P = V$ and $R = U$); $MacTag_V$ is computed by V (and verified by U) using

$MacData_V$ = "KC_2_V" $\| ID_V \| ID_U \| EphemPubKey_V \| EphemPubKey_U \{\| Text_1\}$.

Party U provides $MacTag_U$ to V (as specified in Section 8.2, with $P = U$ and $R = V$); $MacTag_U$ is computed by U (and verified by V) using

$MacData_U$ = "KC_2_U" $\| ID_U \| ID_V \| EphemPubKey_U \| EphemPubKey_V \{\| Text_2\}$.

Note that in Figure 11, party V's ephemeral public key ($EphemPubKey_V$) and the *MacTag* ($MacTag_V$) are depicted as being sent in the same message (to reduce the number of passes in the combined key agreement/key confirmation process). They may also be sent separately and if sent separately, then the order in which the *MacTags* are sent could be reversed.

8.4.4 C(1, 2) Scheme with Unilateral Key Confirmation Provided by U to V

Figure 12 depicts a typical flow for a C(1, 2) scheme with unilateral key confirmation from U to V. In this situation, party U, the scheme initiator, and party V, the scheme responder, assume the roles of key confirmation provider and recipient, respectively. Since V does not contribute an ephemeral public key during the key agreement process, a nonce (*Nonce$_V$*) **shall** be provided to U prior to the computation of the *MacTag* and used as the *EphemData$_V$* during *MacTag* computations. The successful completion of the key confirmation process provides party V with assurance that party U has derived the same secret Z value. If *Nonce$_V$* is a *random nonce* (see Section 5.4), then party V also obtains assurance that party U has actively participated in the process.

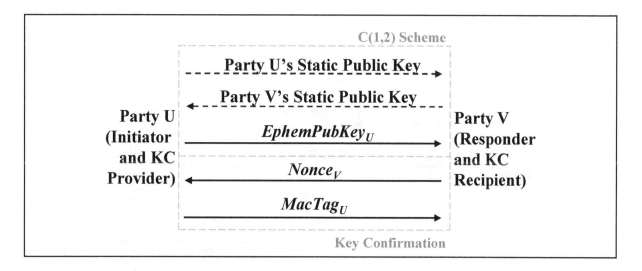

Figure 12: C(1, 2) Scheme with Unilateral Key Confirmation from Party U to Party V

To provide (and receive) key confirmation (as described in Section 8.2), U (and V) set *EphemData$_U$* = *EphemPubKey$_U$*, and *EphemData$_V$* = *Nonce$_V$*:

Party U provides *MacTag$_U$* to V (as specified in Section 8.2, with *P* = *U* and *R* = *V*), where *MacTag$_U$* is computed (as specified in Section 5.2.1) using

  MacDataU = "KC_1_U" || *ID$_U$* || *ID$_V$* || *EphemPubKey$_U$* || *Nonce$_V$* {|| *Text*}.

The recipient V uses the same format for *MacData$_U$* to compute its own version of *MacTag$_U$* and then verifies that the newly computed *MacTag* matches the value provided by U.

8.4.5 C(1, 2) Scheme with Unilateral Key Confirmation Provided by V to U

Figure 13 depicts a typical flow for a C(1, 2) scheme with unilateral key confirmation from V to U. In this situation, party V, the scheme responder, and party U, the scheme initiator, assume the roles of key confirmation provider and recipient, respectively. The successful completion of the key confirmation process provides party U with a) assurance that party V has derived the same secret Z value; and b) assurance that party V has actively participated in the process.

To provide (and receive) key confirmation (as described in Section 8.2), both parties set *EphemData$_V$* = *Null*, and *EphemData$_U$* = *EphemPubKey$_U$*:

Party V provides *MacTag$_V$* to U (as specified in Section 8.2, with $P = V$ and $R = U$), where *MacTag$_V$* is computed (as specified in Section 5.2.1) using

MacData$_V$ = "KC_1_V" || *ID$_V$* || *ID$_U$* || *Null* || *EphemPubKey$_U$* {|| *Text*}.

The recipient U uses the same format for *MacData$_V$* to compute its own version of *MacTag$_V$*, and then verifies that the newly computed *MacTag* matches the value provided by V.

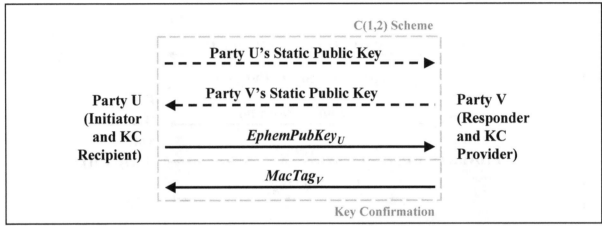

Figure 13: C(1, 2) Scheme with Unilateral Key Confirmation from Party V to Party U

8.4.6 C(1, 2) Scheme with Bilateral Key Confirmation

Figure 14 depicts a typical flow for a C(1, 2) scheme with bilateral key confirmation. In this method, party U, the scheme initiator, and party V, the scheme responder, assume the roles of both the provider and the recipient in order to obtain bilateral key confirmation. V **shall** contribute a nonce (*Nonce$_V$*) prior to U's computation of the *MacTag$_U$*. The successful completion of the key confirmation process provides each party with assurance that the other party has derived the same secret Z value. Party U obtains assurance that party V has actively participated in the process; if *Nonce$_V$* is a *random nonce* (see Section 5.4), then party V also obtains assurance that party U has actively participated in the process.

To provide bilateral key confirmation (as described in Section 8.3), U and V exchange and verify *MacTags* that have been computed (as specified in Sections 5.2.1) using *EphemData$_U$* = *EphemPubKey$_U$* and *EphemData$_V$* = *Nonce$_V$*:

Party V provides MacTag$_V$ to U (as specified in Section 8.2, with $P = V$ and $R = U$); *MacTag$_V$* is computed by V (and verified by U) using

MacData$_V$ = "KC_2_V" || *ID$_V$* || *ID$_U$* || *Nonce$_V$* || *EphemPubKey$_U$* {|| *Text$_1$*}.

Party U provides *MacTag$_U$* to V (as specified in Section 8.2, with $P = U$ and $R = V$); *MacTag$_U$* is computed by U (and verified by V) using

$MacData_U = \text{“KC\_2\_U”} \| ID_U \| ID_V \| EphemPubKey_U \| Nonce_V \{\| Text_2\}.$

Note that in Figure 14, party V's nonce ($Nonce_V$) and the $MacTag$ ($MacTag_V$) are depicted as being sent in the same message (to reduce the number of passes in the combined key agreement/key confirmation process). They may also be sent separately, and if sent separately, then the order in which the $MacTags$ are sent could be reversed.

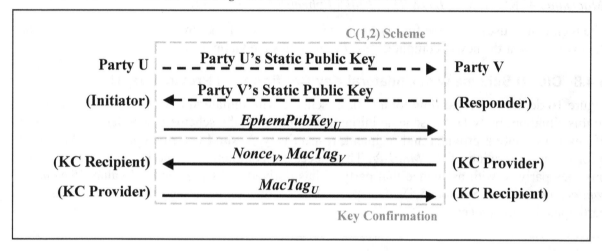

Figure 14: C(1, 2) Scheme with Bilateral Key Confirmation

8.4.7 C(1, 1) Scheme with Unilateral Key Confirmation Provided by V to U

Figure 15 depicts a typical flow for a C(1, 1) scheme with unilateral key confirmation from V to U. In this situation, party V, the scheme responder, and party U, the scheme initiator, assume the roles of key confirmation provider and recipient, respectively. The successful completion of the key confirmation process provides party U with a) assurance that party V has derived the same secret Z value; and b) assurance that party V has actively participated in the process.

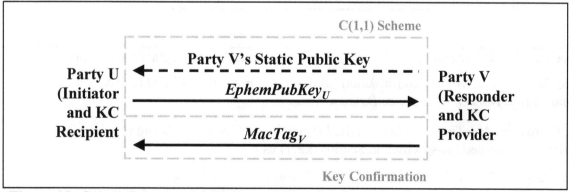

Figure 15: C(1, 1) Scheme with Unilateral Key Confirmation from Party V to Party U

To provide (and receive) key confirmation (as described in Section 8.2), both parties set *EphemData$_V$ = Null*, and *EphemData$_U$ = EphemPubKey$_U$*:

Party V provides *MacTag$_V$* to U (as specified in Section 8.2, with *P = V* and *R = U*), where *MacTag$_V$* is computed (as specified in Section 5.2.1) using

$MacData_V =$ "KC_1_V" $\| ID_V \| ID_U \| Null \| EphemPubKey_U \{\| Text\}$.

The recipient U uses the same format for *MacData$_V$* to compute its own version of *MacTag$_V$* and then verifies that the newly computed *MacTag* matches the value provided by V.

8.4.8 C(0, 2) Scheme with Unilateral Key Confirmation Provided by U to V

Figure 16 depicts a typical flow for a C(0, 2) scheme with unilateral key confirmation from U to V. In this situation, party U, the scheme initiator, and party V, the scheme responder, assume the roles of key confirmation provider and recipient, respectively. V **shall** contribute a nonce (*Nonce$_V$*) to U prior to the generation of the *MacTag*. The successful completion of the key confirmation process provides party V with assurance that party U has derived the same secret Z value. If *Nonce$_V$* is a *random nonce* (see Section 5.4), then party V also obtains assurance that party U has actively participated in the process.

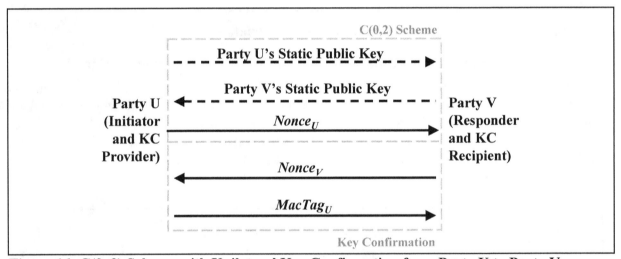

Figure 16: C(0, 2) Scheme with Unilateral Key Confirmation from Party U to Party V

To provide (and receive) key confirmation (as described in Section 8.2), U (and V) set *EphemData$_U$ = Nonce$_U$*, and *EphemData$_V$ = Nonce$_V$*:

Party U provides *MacTag$_U$* to V (as specified in Section 8.2, with *P = U* and *R = V*), where *MacTag$_U$* is computed (as specified in Section 5.2.1) using

$MacData_U =$ "KC_1_U" $\| ID_U \| ID_V \| Nonce_U \| Nonce_V \{\| Text\}$.

The recipient V uses the same format for *MacData$_U$* to compute its own version of *MacTag$_U$* and then verifies that the newly computed *MacTag* matches the value provided by U.

8.4.9 C(0, 2) Scheme with Unilateral Key Confirmation Provided by V to U

Figure 17 depicts a typical flow for a C(0, 2) scheme with unilateral key confirmation from V to U. In this situation, party V, the scheme responder, and party U, the scheme initiator, assume the roles of key confirmation provider and recipient, respectively. The successful completion of the key confirmation process provides party U with assurance that party V has derived the same secret Z value; if $Nonce_U$ is a *random nonce* (see Section 5.4), then party U also obtains assurance that party V has actively participated in the process.

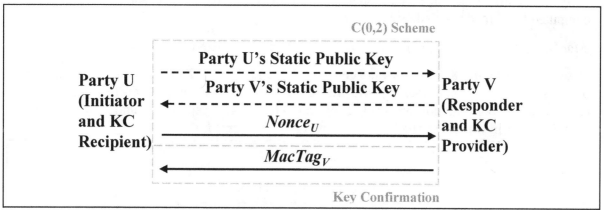

Figure 17: C(0, 2) Scheme with Unilateral Key Confirmation from Party V to Party U

To provide (and receive) key confirmation (as described in Section 8.2), Both parties set $EphemData_V = Null$, and $EphemData_U = Nonce_U$:

Party V provides $MacTag_V$ to U (as specified in 8.2, with $P = V$ and $R = U$), where $MacTag_V$ is computed (as specified in Section 5.2.1) using

$MacData_V =$ "KC_1_V" $\| ID_V \| ID_U \| Null \| Nonce_U \{\| Text\}$.

The recipient U uses the same format for $MacData_V$ to compute its own version of $MacTag_V$, and then verifies that the newly computed $MacTag$ matches the value provided by V.

8.4.10 C(0, 2) Scheme with Bilateral Key Confirmation

Figure 18 depicts a typical flow for a C(0, 2) scheme with bilateral key confirmation. In this method, party U, the scheme initiator, and party V, the scheme responder, assume the roles of both the provider and the recipient in order to obtain bilateral key confirmation. V **shall** contribute a nonce ($Nonce_V$) prior to the generation of $MacTag_U$. The successful completion of the key confirmation process provides each party with assurance that the other party has derived the same secret Z value. If $Nonce_U$ is a *random nonce* (see Section 5.4), then party U obtains assurance that party V has actively participated in the process; if $Nonce_V$ is a *random nonce*, then party V obtains assurance that party U has actively participated in the process.

To provide bilateral key confirmation (as described in Section 8.3), U and V exchange and verify *MacTags* that have been computed (as specified in Sections 5.2.1) using $EphemData_U = Nonce_U$, and $EphemData_V = Nonce_V$:

Party V provides $MacTag_V$ to U (as specified in Section 8.2, with $P = V$ and $R = U$); $MacTag_V$ is computed by V (and verified by U) using

$MacData_V$ = "KC_2_V" || ID_V || ID_U || $Nonce_V$ || $Nonce_U$ {|| $Text_1$}.

Party U provides $MacTag_U$ to V (as specified in Section 8.2, with $P = U$ and $R = V$); $MacTag_U$ is computed by U (and verified by V) using

$MacData_U$ = "KC_2_U" || ID_U || ID_V || $Nonce_U$ || $Nonce_V$ {|| $Text_2$}.

Note that in Figure 18, party V's nonce ($Nonce_V$) and the *MacTag* ($MacTag_V$) are depicted as being sent in the same message (to reduce the number of passes in the combined key agreement/key confirmation process). They may also be sent separately, and if sent separately, then the order in which the *MacTags* are sent could be reversed.

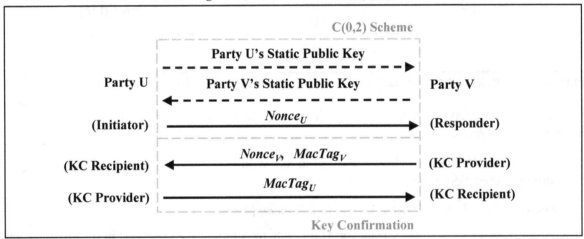

Figure 18: C(0, 2) Scheme with Bilateral Key Confirmation

9. Key Recovery

For some applications, the secret keying material used to protect data may need to be recovered (for example, if the normal reference copy of the secret keying material is lost or corrupted). In this case, either the secret keying material or sufficient information to reconstruct the secret keying material needs to be available (for example, the keys, domain parameters and other inputs to the scheme used to perform the key establishment process).

Keys used during the key establishment process **shall** be handled in accordance with the following:

1. A static key pair **may** be saved.

2. An ephemeral public key **may** be saved.

3. An ephemeral private key **shall** be zeroized after use and, therefore, **shall not** be recoverable.

4. A symmetric key **may** be saved.

Note: This implies that keys derived from schemes where both parties generate ephemeral key pairs (see Section 6.1) cannot be made recoverable by reconstruction of the secret keying material by parties requiring the ephemeral private key in their calculations. For those schemes where only the initiator generates an ephemeral key pair (see Section 6.2), only the responder can recover the secret keying material by reconstruction.

General guidance on key recovery and the protections required for each type of key is provided in the Recommendation for Key Management [7].

10. Implementation Validation

When the NIST Cryptographic Module Validation Program (CMVP) has established a validation program for this Recommendation, a vendor **shall** have its implementation tested and validated by the CMVP in order to claim conformance to this Recommendation. Information on the CMVP is available at http://csrc.nist.gov/cryptval/.

An implementation claiming conformance to this Recommendation **shall** include one or more of the following capabilities:

- Domain parameter generation as specified in Section 5.5.1.

- Explicit domain parameter validation as specified in Section 5.5.2, item 2.

- Key pair generation as specified in Section 5.6.1; documentation **shall** include how assurance of domain parameter validity is expected to be achieved by the key pair owner.

- Explicit public key validation as specified in Section 5.6.2.4 for FFC or as specified in Sections 5.6.2.5 or 5.6.2.6 for ECC.

- A key agreement scheme from Section 6, together with an Approved key derivation function from Section 5.8. Other key derivation methods may be temporarily allowed for backward compatibility. These other allowable methods and any restrictions on their use will be specified in FIPS 140-2 Annex D. If key confirmation is also claimed, the appropriate key confirmation technique from Section 8 **shall** be used. Documentation **shall** include how assurance of private key possession and of assurance of domain parameter and public key validity are expected to be achieved by both the owner and the recipient.

- A key transport scheme as specified in Section 7.

An implementer **shall** also identify the appropriate specifics of the implementation, including:

- The security strength(s) of supported cryptographic algorithms; this will determine the parameter set requirements (see Tables 1 and 2 in Section 5.5.1),

- The domain parameter generation method (see Section 5.5.1).

- The hash function (see Section 5.1),

- The MAC key size(s) (see Tables 1 and 2 in Section 5.5.1),

- The MAC length(s) (see Tables 1 and 2 in Section 5.5.1),

- The type of cryptography: FFC or ECC,

- The key establishment schemes available (see Section 6),

- The key derivation function to be used, including the format of *OtherInfo* (see Section 5.8),

- The type of nonces to be generated (see Section 5.4),

- The NIST Recommended elliptic curve(s) available (if appropriate), and

- The key confirmation scheme (see Section 8).

Appendix A: Summary of Differences between this Recommendation and ANS X9 Standards (Informative)

This list is informational and not meant to be exhaustive, but is intended to summarize important differences between this Recommendation and the indicated ANS X9 standards. In general, this Recommendation can be seen as being more restrictive than the ANS X9 standards, but is derived from them. The list of differences is as follows:

1. ANS X9.42 defines *MacData* for validation testing as "ANSI X9.42 Testing Message". ANS X9.63 does not address implementation validation at this level of detail. Note that the implementation test message used for NIST validation is a different text string from the implementation test message for ANS X9.42; therefore, conformance to the method in this Recommendation does not conform with the ANS X9.42 method. See Section 5.2.3 of this Recommendation for more information.

2. Random generation and validation of FFC and ECC domain parameters are being extended to (a) specify the use of all Approved hash algorithms for generating and validating domain parameters supporting larger key sizes, (b) support the optional use of the Shawe-Taylor algorithm to construct and validate FFC primes and (c) support the verifiably random generation of the generator of the subgroup. See the FIPS 186-3[3] and the ANS X9.62-2[13].

3. For FFC domain parameters: (a) The size of the field order p is limited to either 1024 or 2048 bits, whereas X9.42 allows these sizes along with other multiples of 256 bits that are at least 1024 bits; (b) The size of q (subgroup order) is specified, unlike ANS X9.42 where the size of q has a minimum length of 160 bits; and (c) ANS X9.42 only identifies *SEED* and *pgenCounter* as being among the domain parameters in its Appendix A, but this Recommendation lists them explicitly to be consistent with ANS X9.63. FFC domain parameters that conform to this Recommendation in this area also conform to ANS X9.42, although the reverse is not necessarily true. See Section 5.5.1.1 of this Recommendation for more information.

4. For ECC domain parameters: The cofactor is 32 bits or less, depending on the selected subgroup order, which is more restrictive than ANS X9.63. ECC domain parameters that conform to this Recommendation also conform to ANS X9.63, although the reverse is not necessarily true. See Section 5.5.1.2 of this Recommendation for more information.

5. Some schemes in ANS X9.42 and X9.63 allow one set of domain parameters to be used with static keys and a different set of domain parameters to be used with ephemeral keys in the same scheme. This Recommendation, however, requires the use of only one set of domain parameters in one scheme; that is, the same set of domain parameters is used with the static and ephemeral keys in any given scheme. Therefore, the ANS X9.42 dhHybrid2 scheme is not allowed. See Section 5.5 of this Recommendation for more information.

Also, the ANS X9.63 Combined Unified Model is not allowed, and the ANS X9.63 Station to Station (STS) method is not specified in this Recommendation; STS is a protocol that is based upon the ECC Ephemeral Unified Model scheme and, as a protocol, is not prohibited.

6. Assurances of the arithmetic validity of a public key are required in this Recommendation. Assurance of validity is optional in ANS X9.42, but required in ANS X9.63. In both cases, the means of obtaining that assurance is different than in this Recommendation. See Section 5.6.2 of this Recommendation for more information.

7. ANS X9.63 specifies both cofactor and non-cofactor schemes. For this Recommendation, only ECC cofactor schemes are used. The use of an ECC scheme that conforms to this Recommendation also conforms to ANS X9.63, although the reverse is not necessarily true. See Section 5.7 of this Recommendation for details.

8. Regarding the key derivation function (KDF):

a. This recommendation specifies two Approved KDFs, the concatenation KDF specified in Section 5.8.1 and the ASN.1 KDF specified in Section 5.8.2. Other key derivation methods may be temporarily allowed for backward compatibility. These other allowable methods and any restrictions on their use will be specified in FIPS 140-2 Annex D.

b. ANS X9.42 provides a concatenation KDF and an ASN.1 KDF, while ANS X9.63 provides only the concatenation KDF. However, the Approved KDFs of this Recommendation require that the counter appears before the shared secret as input to the hash function, whereas the ANSI KDFs place the counter after the shared secret

c. The Approved KDFs in this Recommendation require the input of the identifiers of the communicating parties; such information is not required in ANS X9.42 and X9.63.

d. In this Recommendation, the shared secret is zeroized after a single call to a key derivation function, before the key agreement scheme releases any portion of the *DerivedKeyingMaterial* for use by relying applications.. The ANS X9.42 and X9.63 standards do not indicate when the shared secret needs to be zeroized. An implication of this Recommendation's requirement concerning zeroization is that all of the keying material directly derived from the shared secret must be computed during one call to the KDF.

9. FFC and ECC key transport use an Approved key-wrapping algorithm, such as the AES key-wrapping algorithm. ANS X9.63 specifies the ECIES method, which is not allowed in this Recommendation. Therefore, the use of a key transport method that conforms to this Recommendation does **not** conform to the method in ANS X9.63. See Section 7 of this Recommendation for details. ANS X9.42 does not specify a key transport method.

10. There is a comprehensive specification in this Recommendation of approved ways to do key confirmation (KC) when KC is desired as part of the key establishment process. See Section 8 of this Recommendation for details. Key confirmation is not discussed in ANS X9.42, but a few examples of key confirmation are provided in ANS X9.63.

11. This Recommendation specifies that an ephemeral key is used for exactly one transaction, with the exception that the sender may use the same ephemeral key pair in multiple DLC-based Key Transport transactions if the same secret keying material is being transported in each transaction and if all these transactions occur "simultaneously" (or within a short period of time). ANS X9.42 and X9.63 do not allow this exception.

Appendix B: Rationale for Including Identifiers in the KDF Input

In this Recommendation, it is required that identifiers for both parties to a key agreement transaction be included in the *OtherInfo* that is input to the key derivation function. (See Sections 5.8.1 and 5.8.2.)

The inclusion of sufficiently-specific identifiers for the initiator (U) and responder (V) provides assurance that the keying material derived by U and V will be different from the keying material that is derived by other parties (or by the same parties acting in opposite roles). As a result, key agreement schemes gain resilience against unknown key share attacks, which depend on some type of confusion over the role played by each party (initiator versus responder). (See, for example, references [14], [15], [16], and [17], which all recommend the inclusion of identifiers in the KDF as a means of eliminating certain vulnerabilities.)

In addition to identifiers for the initiator and responder, the inclusion of additional context-specific information in *OtherInfo* can be used to draw finer distinctions between key agreement transactions, providing assurance that parties will not derive the same keying material unless they agree on all the included information. Examples of additional context-specific information include the intended use of the derived keying material, the choice of key agreement scheme used to produce the shared secret Z, ephemeral public keys or nonces exchanged during the transaction, and session numbers.

Appendix C: Data Conversions (Normative)

C.1 Integer-to-Byte String Conversion

Input: A non-negative integer C and the intended length n of the byte string satisfying

$$2^{8n} > C$$

When called from an FFC Scheme, $n = \lceil t/8 \rceil$ bytes, where $t = \lceil \log_2 p \rceil$ where p is the large prime field order.

Output: A byte string S of length n bytes.

1. Let $S_1, S_2,..., S_n$ be the bytes of S from leftmost to rightmost.

2. The bytes of S **shall** satisfy:

$$C = \sum 2^{8(n-i)} S_i \text{ for } i = 1 \text{ to } n.$$

C.2 Field-Element-to-Byte String Conversion

Input: An element α in the field F_q.

Output: A byte string S of length $n = \lceil t/8 \rceil$ bytes, where $t = \lceil \log_2 q \rceil$.

1. If q is an odd prime, then α must be an integer in the interval $[0, q-1]$; α **shall** be converted to a byte string of length n bytes using the technique specified in Appendix C.1 above.

2. If $q = 2^m$, then α must be a bit string of length m bits. Let $s_1, s_2, ..., s_m$ be the bits of α from leftmost to rightmost. Let $S_1, S_2, ..., S_n$ be the bytes of S from leftmost to rightmost. The rightmost bit s_m **shall** become the rightmost bit of the last byte S_n, and so on through the leftmost bit s_1, which **shall** become the $(8n - m + 1)^{\text{th}}$ bit of the first byte S_1. The leftmost $(8n - m)$ bits of the first byte S_1 **shall** be zero.

C.3 Field-Element-to-Integer Conversion

Input: An element α in the field F_q.

Output: An integer x.

1. If q is an odd prime, then $x = \alpha$ (no conversion is required).

2. If $q = 2^m$, then α must be a bit string of length m bits. Let $s_1, s_2, ..., s_m$ be the bits of α from leftmost to rightmost. α **shall** be converted to an integer x satisfying:

$$x = \sum 2^{(m-i)} s_i \qquad \text{for } i = 1 \text{ to } m.$$

Appendix D: References (Informative)

[1]   FIPS 140-2, Security requirements for Cryptographic Modules, May 25, 2001.

[2]   FIPS 180-2, Secure Hash Standard, August 2002.

[3]   FIPS 186-3, Digital Signature Standard, anticipated in 2006

[4]   FIPS 197, Advanced Encryption Standard, November 2001.

[5]   FIPS 198, The Keyed-Hash Message Authentication Code (HMAC), March 2002.

[6]   NIST SP 800-38B, Recommendation for Block Cipher Modes of Operation: The CMAC Mode for Authentication, May 2005.

[7]   NIST SP 800-57, Recommendation for Key Management, August 2005.

[8]   AES Key Wrap Specification, NIST, November 16, 2001.

[9]   ANS X9.31-1998, Digital Signatures Using Reversible Public Key Cryptography for the Financial Services Industry (rDSA).

[10]   ANS X9.42-2001, Public Key Cryptography for the Financial Services Industry: Agreement of Symmetric Keys Using Discrete Logarithm Cryptography.

[11]   ANS X9.44 (Draft), Public Key Cryptography for the Financial Services Industry: Key Establishment Using Integer Factorization Cryptography, December 2002.

[12]   ANS X9.63-2001, Public Key Cryptography for the Financial Services Industry: Key Agreement and Key Transport Using Elliptic Curve Cryptography.

[13]   ANS X9.62-2 Elliptic Curve Digital Signature Algorithm (ECDSA), November 16, 2005.

[14]   On Session Key Construction in Provably-Secure Key Establishment Protocols, Kim-Kwang Raymond Choo, Colin Boyd, and Yvonne Hitchcock, LNCS, Vol. 3715, pp. 116-131, Springer-Verlag, 2005. Extended version available at: http://eprint.iacr.org/2005/206.pdf.

[15]   Another Look at HMQV Alfred Menezes, Nov. 2005. Available at: http://eprint. iacr.org/2005/205.pdf.

[16]   Evaluation of Security Level of Cryptography: ECMQVS (from SEC 1), Phillip Rogaway, Mihir Bellare, Dan Boneh, Jan. 2001. Available at: http://www.ipa.go.jp/security/enc/CRYPTREC/fy15/doc/1069_ks-ecmqv.pdf.

[17]   Unknown Key-Share Attacks on the Station-to-Station (STS) Protocol, Simon Blake-Wilson, Alfred Menezes, Technical Report CORR 98-42, University of Waterloo, 1998. Available at: http://cacr.math.uwaterloo.ca.

Appendix E: Revisions (Informative)

The original version of this document was published in March, 2006. In March, 2007, the following revision was made to allow the dual use of keys during certificate requests:

In Section 5.6.4.2, the second item was originally as follows:

"A static key pair may be used in more than one key establishment scheme. However, one static public/private key pair **shall not** be used for different purposes (for example, a digital signature key pair is not to be used for key establishment or vice versa)."

The item was changed to the following, where the changed text is indicated in italics:

"A static key pair may be used in more than one key establishment scheme. However, one static public/private key pair **shall not** be used for different purposes (for example, a digital signature key pair is not to be used for key establishment or vice versa) *with the following possible exception: when requesting the (initial) certificate for a public static key establishment key, the key establishment private key associated with the public key may be used to sign the certificate request. See SP 800-57, Part 1 on Key Usage for further information.*"

www.ingramcontent.com/pod-product-compliance
Lightning Source LLC
Chambersburg PA
CBHW080430060326
40689CB00019B/4447